WITHDRAWN
FROM THE VPI & SU
LIBRARY COLLECTION

Reaching across the Waters

D1714721

Reaching across the Waters

Facing the Risks of Cooperation in International Waters

Ashok Subramanian
Bridget Brown
Aaron Wolf

THE WORLD BANK
Washington, D.C.

WATER
PARTNERSHIP
PROGRAM

© 2012 International Bank for Reconstruction and Development/The World Bank
1818 H Street NW
Washington DC 20433
Telephone: 202-473-1000
Internet: www.worldbank.org

Some rights reserved

1 2 3 4 15 14 13 12

This work is a product of the staff of The World Bank with external contributions. Note that The World Bank does not necessarily own each component of the content included in the work. The World Bank therefore does not warrant that the use of the content contained in the work will not infringe on the rights of third parties. The risk of claims resulting from such infringement rests solely with you.

The findings, interpretations, and conclusions expressed in this work do not necessarily reflect the views of The World Bank, its Board of Executive Directors, or the governments they represent. The World Bank does not guarantee the accuracy of the data included in this work. The boundaries, colors, denominations, and other information shown on any map in this work do not imply any judgment on the part of The World Bank concerning the legal status of any territory or the endorsement or acceptance of such boundaries.

Nothing herein shall constitute or be considered to be a limitation upon or waiver of the privileges and immunities of The World Bank, all of which are specifically reserved.

Rights and Permissions

This work is available under the Creative Commons Attribution 3.0 Unported license (CC BY 3.0) http://creativecommons.org/licenses/by/3.0. Under the Creative Commons Attribution license, you are free to copy, distribute, transmit, and adapt this work, including for commercial purposes, under the following conditions:

Attribution—Please cite the work as follows: Subramanian, Ashok, Bridget Brown, and Aaron Wolf. 2012. *Reaching across the Waters: Facing the Risks of Cooperation in International Waters.* Washington, DC: World Bank. DOI. 10.1596/978-0-8213-9594-3 License: Creative Commons Attribution CC BY 3.0

Translations—If you create a translation of this work, please add the following disclaimer along with the attribution: *This translation was not created by The World Bank and should not be considered an official World Bank translation. The World Bank shall not be liable for any content or error in this translation.*

All queries on rights and licenses should be addressed to the Office of the Publisher, The World Bank, 1818 H Street NW, Washington, DC 20433, USA; fax: 202-522-2625; e-mail: pubrights@worldbank.org.

ISBN (paper): 978-0-8213-9594-3
ISBN (electronic): 978-0-8213-9595-0
DOI (print): 10.1596/978-0-8213-9594-3

Cover photo: Leonard Abrams
Cover design: Naylor Design, Washington, D.C.

Library of Congress Cataloging-in-Publication Data
Subramanian, Ashok, 1950-
  Reaching across the waters : facing the risks of cooperation in international waters / Ashok Subramanian, Bridget Brown, and Aaron Wolf.
     p. cm.
  Includes bibliographical references.
  ISBN 978-0-8213-9594-3 — ISBN 978-0-8213-9595-0 (electronic)
  1. Water-supply—Management—International cooperation. 2. Water resources development—International cooperation. I. Brown, Bridget. II. Wolf, Aaron T. III. Title.
  HD1691.S823 2012
  333.91—dc23

                                                                      2012017466

Contents

Maps

Figures Framework:

Tables

Foreword

Water can be a source of conflict, but it can also serve the goals of cooperation. Indeed, cooperation over shared waters has averted many approaching conflicts. But there is no guarantee that the future will be an extension of the past. Recent analyses of global and regional security and conflicts have alerted us to new and emerging threats to a cooperative future.

The World Bank and its partners have recognized the values of supporting countries' desires for cooperative action in shared international waters, beginning with the 1960 Indus Waters Treaty. Interest and involvement in international waters have only grown since. There were 123 World Bank–funded projects with activities related to international waterways between 1997 and 2007, 40 of which were financed by grants from the Global Environmental Facility (GEF). Close to 100 projects were ongoing in 2010. The amounts committed to transboundary projects were US$6.2 billion, primarily in International Development Association and International Bank for Reconstruction and Development funding, and US$273.5 million in GEF grants. The tradition of support has extended over the years—from engagement in the Indus to the Mekong; the Baltic Sea and Danube; the Aral Sea; the Guarani Aquifer; and to the Nile, Niger, and Senegal.

The economic benefits of river basin cooperation are many. Yet, there have been constraints to countries seeking cooperation deals and challenges facing development partners engaged in shared river basins. Recent reviews have highlighted the need for a better understanding of the political economy of cooperation, both on the part of countries and of partners.

I am delighted that a dedicated team of experienced staff members, together with expert advisers, has put together an evidence-based and applications-oriented volume on cooperation in international waters. I am certain that the perspectives on political risks and opportunities and the authors' advice on various risk reduction measures will help the leaders and teams to vigorously promote cooperation and prevent potential conflicts.

Julia Bucknall
Manager, Water Anchor
The World Bank

About the Authors

Ashok Subramanian is a water resources management specialist based in Virginia. As a water management specialist for over 20 years, he has led and promoted the application of country and transboundary level analysis, investments, and action in countries and river basins across the world. Most recently, as an adviser in the World Bank's Water Anchor, he led a major study on cooperation in international waters. He has graduate degrees from the Indian Institute of Management, Ahmedabad, and Princeton University, New Jersey, and he has broad experience in rural and water development policies and programs. He is the author of several papers and reports on water resource management and water institutions.

Bridget Brown earned an M.S. in water resources policy and management in 2010 at Oregon State University. Her graduate research focused on water policy in the Middle East and North Africa, as well as water conflict management in the western United States. Prior to collaborating on this study, she worked as a research assistant for two projects funded by the United States Agency for International Development (USAID) and for the Oregon Sea Grant as a climate engagement coordinator. She is currently the coordinator for the University of Wisconsin–Milwaukee's forthcoming master's degree program in sustainable peacebuilding.

Aaron Wolf is a professor of geography at the College of Earth, Ocean, and Atmospheric Sciences at Oregon State University, Corvallis. He has an M.S. in water resources management (emphasizing hydrogeology) and a Ph.D. in environmental policy analysis (emphasizing dispute resolution) from the University of Wisconsin, Madison. His research focuses on issues relating transboundary water resources to political conflict and cooperation. He is a trained mediator and facilitator and directs the Program in Water Conflict Management and Transformation, through which he has offered workshops, facilitations, and mediation in basins throughout the world. He developed and coordinates the Transboundary Freshwater Dispute Database at Oregon State University, Corvallis.

Acknowledgments

Acknowledging our debt is like making the acceptance speech at the Oscars. The minutes are ticking by, and you are not sure if you have thanked everyone who helped you get there. And then, the words never quite convey the depth of appreciation of the many contributions. But we will try. Please stop the music.

J. B. Collier, Washington, D.C., participated at key points in the study with helpful advice and carried the administrative burdens. Contributions, including writing and discussions, from the case study authors were invaluable to our analysis. For this work, we would like to sincerely thank Barbara Miller, Eileen Burke, and J. B. Collier (Eastern Nile); Claudia Sadoff and Brendan Galipeau (Ganges); Aminou Tassiou, Audace Ndayizeye, J. B. Collier, and Amal Talbi (Niger); Daryl Fields, Simon Croxton, Martha Jarosewich-Holder, Alfred Diebold, and Frank Schrader (Syr Darya); and Marcus Wishart, Thomas Bernauer, and Lucas Beck (Zambezi). Their interest in taking the study beyond analysis to operational action was truly gratifying.

Lada Turbina and Thembi Kumapley, in the Africa Region of the World Bank, provided just the right support at the right time for the teleconferences and contracts. Guy Alaerts, Daryl Fields, Barbara Miller, Claudia Sadoff, and Susanne Schmeier served as peer reviewers and provided excellent feedback. Other colleagues and friends extended enormous support in their own ways: Len Abrams, Herbert Acquay, Sameer Ahmed, Vahid Alavian, Thomas Bernauer, Louise Croneborg, Charles Di Leva, Ousmane Dione, Inez Dombrowsky, Al Duda, Nina Eejima, Jakob Granit, David Grey, Nagarajarao Harshdeep, Michael Jacobsen, Vijay Jagannathan, Saroj Jha, Torkil Jonch Clausen, Jonathan Kamkwalala, Karin Kemper, Christina Leb, Stephen Lintner, Shelley McMillan, Halla Quaddumi, Jamal Saghir, Gustavo Saltiel, Winston Yu, and Ivan Zavadsky. They offered advice, comments, and inputs via e-mail at the concept and final review meetings and over phone, lunches, and coffees. The final version is the better for it. Jeff Lecksell extended a thorough assessment of the maps to ensure compliance. The usual caveat applies: all of the above are to be credited for the strengths, while the authors have to account for the final product and any gaps.

We learned a lot from the many discussions and debates with partners at various water events across the globe, at trust fund meetings, and through one-on-one exchanges. Their commitment to collaboration over water and among external development partners was inspiring.

Julia Bucknall was a generous host as manager of the Water Anchor where Ashok Subramanian was an adviser. She showed keen interest at each stage of development. The Water Anchor was a delightful setting for the analysis and writing. The Bank's Institutional Staff Resources Program enabled Ashok Subramanian to spend a significant part of his time during 2012 on the study and deserves much appreciation.

Funding support from the Water Partnership Program (WPP) made the study possible. Diego Rodriguez, Matthijs Schuring, and Peggy Johnston of the WPP helped to translate our interests into action through carefully vetted proposals and queries.

Inger Andersen, now regional vice president, Middle East and North Africa Region of the World Bank, was an inspiration and mentor. Her interest and expertise in international waters brought the formative idea to fruition, and for that she deserves special recognition. Her questions, based on rich experience in regional cooperation and intellectual curiosity, served to sharpen the analysis and writing.

To Uma, big thanks for unfailing support and cheering from the sidelines all the way.

Abbreviations

ATP	Applied Training Project
BCM	billion cubic meters
ECOWAS	Economic Community of West African States
ENSAP	Eastern Nile Subsidiary Action Program
ENTRO	Eastern Nile Technical Regional Office
FAO	Food and Agriculture Organization
GEF	Global Environment Facility
GWP	Global Water Partnership
IHP	International Hydrological Programme
ILC	International Law Commission
IIL	International Institute of Law
IIMI	International Irrigation Management Institute
ILA	International Law Association
IP	investment plan
IW	international waters
IWMI	International Water Management Institute
IWRM	integrated water resources management
NBA	Niger Basin Authority
SAARC	South Asian Association for Regional Cooperation
SADC	Southern African Development Community

SDAP	Sustainable Development Action Plan
SIWI	Stockholm International Water Institute
TA	technical assistance
TFDD	Transboundary Freshwater Dispute Database
UN	United Nations
UNDP	UN Development Programme
UNEP	UN Environment Programme
UNESCO	UN Educational, Scientific and Cultural Organization
USAID	United States Agency for International Development
WPP	Water Partnership Program
WSSD	World Summit on Sustainable Development
WWAP	World Water Assessment Program
WWC	World Water Council
ZAMCOM	Zambezi Watercourse Commission Agreement

Overview

This study reviews the experience of cooperation in five international river basins, focusing on the perceptions of risks and opportunities by decision makers responding to a specific prospect of cooperation. For each basin, the analysis centered on "tipping points" or periods when policy makers in the respective countries face a critical decision concerning water cooperation. The use of historical events helped to avoid the risk that the analyses would affect current negotiations or controversies. River basins selected for the analysis were the Eastern Nile, Ganges, Niger, Syr Darya, and Zambezi.

This study was inspired, in part, by the intensified involvement of the World Bank and its development partners in shared international waters, resulting in a growing interest to better understand the political economy surrounding regional cooperation deals over water. While the associated economic benefits and costs of cooperation are generally well analyzed, the perceptions of decision makers regarding political risks and opportunities have been much less thoroughly explored. Responding to this knowledge gap, this study looks at the political dimension of cooperation over international waters, beginning with perceived risks. Perceived risks are actually a core consideration for country decision makers. Figure O.1 illustrates how countries considering cooperation might incorporate risk

Figure O.1   Framework: Risks and Opportunities to Cooperation

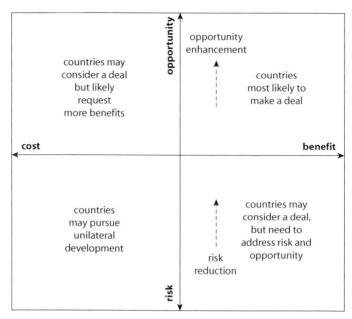

Note: Countries considering cooperation assess their positions on the x-axis in terms of net benefits (benefits less costs) and on the y-axis in terms of net opportunities (opportunities less risks). Benefits and costs are economic, while opportunities and risks are political. Country positions in the framework may determine the likelihood of cooperation in that given situation, as described in the text in each quadrant. Risk reduction and opportunity enhancement (gray arrows) will ideally shift country positions north in the framework.

and opportunity into their decision making. In the upper right quadrant, countries see more opportunity than risk and more benefit than cost.

This study is primarily aimed at external development partners. Countries and individuals engaged in international waters issues may also find this study and its reflections helpful in enhancing their knowledge and advancing their action with respect to regional cooperation.

Perceived Risk

If a country cannot find a way to compensate for or control risk, it may choose not to enter into a cooperative agreement. Hesitation, or even resistance, observed on the part of countries regarding cooperation with other riparian countries can be better understood by evaluating the perceived risks of their engagement. We define perceived risk for a given country as *the perception that an act of cooperation will expose the country to harm, will jeopardize something of value to the country, or will threaten the political future of individual policy makers.*

There appear to be five general categories of risk perceived by decision makers (table O.1). These risk categories were developed through a review of literature on international negotiation and cooperation. In each of the cases, the analysis focused on risks associated with these five broad categories, examining how these risks influenced decision makers and how the risks affected the outcomes of negotiations.

These risks indeed exerted an influence on cooperation decisions. There were commonalities among the countries, yet each case differed in both the context surrounding the risks and also in the type of dominant risks. In some cases, co-riparians perceived similar risks; in other cases, the risks for each country were very different. In addition, sovereignty and equity appeared to be *core* risks in that they were deep-seated, and they tended to resurface, even after deals were made and benefits were delivered.

- In experiencing the **capacity and knowledge** risk, countries feared that they would be at a disadvantage. This risk manifested itself in two major ways:
  - Countries perceived they had less negotiating capacity than their co-riparians.
  - Countries perceived they did not have adequate or accurate information about the basin.

Table O.1   Five Categories of Risk

Capacity and knowledge
Confidence in ability to negotiate a fair deal; having enough and the correct information and knowledge to do so

Accountability and voice
Deliverability of benefits by the regional entity and co-riparians, often related to trust; having a say in decision making in the governing structures of the regional entity

Sovereignty and autonomy
Ability to act in the best interest of the country without constraints; making decisions independently

Equity and access
Fairness of relative benefits to country, including timing of benefits and costs and obtaining and retaining fair access to river

Stability and support
Longevity potential of the agreement; in-country support of the agreement, including the likelihood of ratification

- Decision makers generally experienced the **accountability and voice** risk in regard to the following:
  - Fear that co-riparians, third parties, or the regional institution may not deliver benefits
  - Concern that the respective country's interests would not be adequately considered in joint decision-making processes
  - Perception of a high probability that the regional institutional arrangement would not result in the flow of benefits.
- To a greater or lesser extent, all of the cases reflected the significant risk of **sovereignty and autonomy**. At its core, this risk is about a decision maker sensing the danger of intrusion into the country's authority to make sovereign decisions. It refers to both of the following:
  - The desire to have control over national development goals and related development of resources and infrastructure
  - The right to make decisions independently.
- Countries were acutely concerned with the risk of **equity and access**:
  - Fairness in any deal, regarding specified quantity or quality of water, benefit flows, or project costs
  - Entitlement to use the river. Some countries viewed entitlement as the right to continuing with historic uses; others as gaining access to a river running through (or originating in) its territory; and yet others viewed it as attaining benefits in proportion to a country's relative size in (or percent contribution to) the basin.
- The risk of **stability and support** had direct national and personal implications. It was an important consideration for all countries, but particularly so for countries with diversified and powerful stakeholders. It applied to both of the following:
  - The implementability of an agreement due to the presence or absence of key stakeholder support
  - A decision maker's positive or negative public image. We found this risk to be an important consideration for all countries, but particularly so in countries with diversified and powerful stakeholders.

Enhancing Cooperation

Measures to address these risks were critical in moving to cooperation. *Risk reduction* was an important process in many cases before countries would progress to negotiated outcomes. In some cases, reduced risks provided sufficient motivation for countries to reconsider the cooperation deal, and even sign an agreement. The cases reflected seven broad categories of risk reduction (table O.2):

Political opportunity was also a critical factor in enhancing cooperation in many cases. At times, the perception of resulting national and regional political gains even trumped residual risk. In other words, with sufficient political opportunity, some countries were willing to cooperate even with some risks. Examples of such opportunities from our case studies included shifts in regional politics (favoring solidarity over unilateralism); changes in national leadership that brought in champions willing to take new initiatives on cooperation; and the possibility that cooperation over water between countries could signal or lead to cooperation on other issues in regional and global forums.

Third parties, such as the World Bank and development partners, could play important roles in supporting countries with risk reduction. Examples of such assistance included engaging with countries at an appropriate scale (for example, the entire basin, sub-basin, or country level); conducting detailed risk assessments; designing risk reduction strategies, including financing and guarantees to target dominant risks; and periodically reassessing the risk situation, employing new strategies as

Table O.2   Seven Categories of Risk Reduction

Knowledge and skill expansion
Providing training and studies to meet gaps in capacity and knowledge, and providing support for developing new skills

Institutional design
Tailoring the institutional arrangement to be a "fit for purpose" cooperative arrangement for dialogue and action among riparians

Agreement design
Tailoring the agreement to the preferences of political leaders involved in terms of its formality, scope, goals, and obligations

Program design
Shaping the program to address country interests and goals, including sectoral links, long-term versus short-term benefits, and review and monitoring

Financing and guarantee
Meeting financing needs and gaps identified by countries, including third-party guarantee of financial obligations

Facilitation (third party)
Providing unbiased, third-party assistance in dialogues among riparians, including clarifications and interpretations

Decision legitimacy
Using consultation and discussion forums and other avenues for ensuring widespread domestic and regional support of decisions

needed. The role of partners with respect to political opportunity is less clear and is an area for further research. Meanwhile, partners are encouraged to (a) stay abreast of regional geopolitics in order to be ready if and when opportunities are presented, and (b) continue to implement appropriate risk reduction strategies so that risks have already been dealt with to the extent possible, if and when opportunities are presented.

Key Messages

This study offers several key messages for those engaged in work on cooperation in international waters.

1. **Risks are less studied but are critical in decision making.** Several previous studies have focused on the economic benefits and costs to cooperation over water. Although more recent work has explored expanded benefits that can result from cooperation, less attention has been paid to the role of political economy in decision making and country perception of risks. Thus, this study addresses an important gap in knowledge on the topic of international waters.

2. **Countries are not unitary actors; several stakeholders are likely to be involved.** Sometimes, use of the term "country decision making" can imply that a country is a unitary actor, thereby losing the diversity of interests within a country. It is important to recognize in studies and engagement in international waters that dynamics within each country influence the likelihood of cooperation. Stakeholder voices and the national discourse on cooperation are critical elements in the decision-making process.

3. **Individual decision makers matter; champions are key.** At times, it is the vision, will, charisma, or personal politics of a certain decision maker in a country that determines whether or not a deal is made. Hence, the motives of individual decision makers matter. By extension, partners and teams also matter as they set out to facilitate and support the cooperation process.

4. **Solutions must be devised for situations and should match country needs.** There is no blueprint or one-size-fits-all approach, especially in matters of regional programs, institutional arrangements, and

agreements that will ensure success. Countries take different paths to cooperation. For partners, it is imperative to invest the necessary time and resources to produce the most appropriate solution possible for the situation at hand. Fit-for-purpose remedies rather than "model" river basin solutions are needed.

5. **Risks will most likely require a diversity of interventions.** It will typically take more than a single action to reduce a given risk. A creative and diverse approach is recommended, usually one requiring a mix of interventions. This need is a sound rationale for coordination of partner actions, since no one party can extend support on multiple fronts.

6. **Opportunities can outweigh residual risks.** Even if risks remain, countries may cooperate if certain political opportunities or gains become apparent. Opportunity is a powerful factor in determining the outcome of a cooperation offer. This is an area for further study.

7. **Politics are difficult to predict, so anticipation is critical.** Laying the foundation for cooperation by reducing risks will prepare countries for deals. For partners engaging countries in cooperation, staying abreast of regional geopolitics is important, so that when the time is ripe for cooperation, action can be taken.

8. **National, regional, and global events all affect opportunities.** Changes at any scale can create or change opportunity.

9. **Long-term commitment is needed.** Cooperation takes several years of planning, facilitation, and confidence building, often before formal negotiations even begin.

10. **Deals are dynamic.** Once an agreement is reached, the situation does not become static. Deals can be fragile and fall apart, or they can evolve and grow into stronger and more sustainable arrangements. Accordingly, periodic assessments are needed to reflect a proper diagnosis of current realities and respond with appropriate solutions for situations.

CHAPTER 1

Introduction and Approach

Justification

This study reviews the experience of cooperation in selected international river basins[1] and during selected time periods in those basins. The review is from a country perspective and focuses on the countries' perceived risks and opportunities in engaging in regional cooperation deals in response to the prospects for cooperation. It is primarily aimed at external development partners who promote regional public goods (river basin institutions and agreements) and support cooperative activities and investments in international waters. We also believe that countries and individuals engaged in international waters issues will find this study and reflections helpful in enhancing their knowledge and advancing their actions with respect to regional cooperation. The specific purpose of the study is to alert teams engaged in promoting cooperation in international waters to the need for a careful risk analysis and for the formulation of a risk reduction strategy to help countries move toward cooperation.

The World Bank has a keen interest in this topic. Together with partners, the World Bank has been active in international waters for decades, since its involvement in the Indus Waters Treaty (1960). This engagement has intensified since the 1993 Water Resources Management Policy (World Bank 1993) that advocated a basin approach to water

9

management and the Water Resources Sector Strategy (World Bank 2003) that emphasized a revitalization of water resources development along with improved management. The World Bank's support has been extended to international rivers, lakes, aquifers, and regional seas. Teams have gained valuable experience from such work in engaging countries and partners.

However, the World Bank and its partners have faced several constraints in their engagement in international waters. The World Bank Group Implementation Progress Report of the Water Resources Sector Strategy (commonly called the Mid Cycle Review) highlighted many of these constraints and observed: "Understanding the political economy dimensions of transboundary engagement through upstream analytical work, and technical assistance are critical in reducing the risk profile of investment projects" (World Bank 2010a: 20). This study, focused on international rivers, responds to this concern by drawing on the lessons of international waters from the perspectives of countries facing risks in engaging in cooperation and attempts to identify potential risk reduction strategies.

Background

Water Conflict and Cooperation

Water management, by definition, is conflict management. Water, unlike other consumable resources that are scarce, fuels all parts of society, from biologies to economies to aesthetics and spiritual practices. Moreover, it fluctuates—sometimes wildly—in space and time; its management is usually fragmented; and it is often subject to strongly held beliefs and values and vaguely defined and varying legal principles.

It stands to reason, then, that often water cannot be managed for a single purpose. Water management has multiple objectives and is based on reconciling co-existing and competing interests. Within a nation, these interests include domestic and industrial users, agriculturalists, hydropower generators, tourism and recreation beneficiaries, and environmentalists—any two of whom may be at odds. The complexity of finding mutually acceptable solutions increases with the number of stakeholders involved. When international boundary issues are factored in, the difficulty grows substantially yet again.

This situation has led some to proclaim that water, not oil, is the next battleground.[2] Such statements distort the current reality in which small-scale disputes persist but widespread conflicts over water have rarely, if ever, occurred. Experience and research have found that where the institutional capacity for dialogue and the management of disputes are present, conflict is less likely.[3] Additionally, joint development of a shared river has been shown to increase the sustainability of the resource and help the needs and interests of all countries involved. Cooperation over international waters is thus seen as an important step in both securing regional peace and enhancing sustainable development.

Cooperation over shared waters also promises other substantial benefits, such as the following:

- Access to external markets, leading to economies of scale, for example, lower marginal cost of unit power production in the case of hydropower
- The possibility of building on the comparative advantage of countries, for example, in irrigation or hydropower
- Improved management and coordinated operation of water infrastructure to accommodate multipurpose uses of water
- The possibility of jointly facing common external threats, for example, climate risks or malaria
- The optimal location of infrastructure, for example, leading to potential savings in evaporation losses.

A growing literature documents the many benefits of cooperative action, despite the substantial costs that often accompany the benefits.[4]

Yet, countries are slow to cooperate. If benefits to cooperation are so attractive, as many studies and the economic analyses suggest, substantial regional cooperation over water should be expected. But that is not the current reality, at least not in terms of formal cooperation, for example, with an agreement in place. We find basins all over the world where formal cooperation between co-riparians is lacking or even obstructed by one party or another. Of the world's 276 international basins, 166 have no treaty provisions covering them whatsoever (TFDD 2011). Moreover, many multilateral basins are governed by bilateral treaties—only one-third of the multilateral basins are entirely covered by treaty provisions, and most of those are bilateral (TFDD 2011)—precluding the integrated basin management advocated by water policy experts.

Country Drivers

It is clear why cooperation is considered beneficial in the abstract, as it can lead to the highly desirable goals of sustainable development and integrated water resources management at the level of the river basin. But the critical question is: what drives countries to enter into a deal?

Internal drivers. Developing countries face a set of critical development challenges, opportunities, and constraints. In response, they formulate plans to achieve their broad development goals, such as poverty alleviation and increased competitiveness. These goals call for strategies of increasing incomes, improving access, expanding markets, and building human and social capital.[5] A central means of accomplishing these goals and strategies is achieving food, water, and energy security.

The pressing need for achieving food, water, and energy security goals drives countries to search for solutions through water development.

Countries typically begin with national plans, at times relying on knowledge and financing assistance from development partners; they may then follow such plans with regional plans and partnerships. Regional production centers of food and energy as well as regional markets are seen as attractive means of meeting national goals and are often a lower cost option for countries. Regional power pools are projected to reduce electricity costs by US$2 billion a year by tapping into cost-effective sources of energy in Africa (World Bank 2010b: 143). Many of the studies on regional integration and cooperation present these options as invaluable ways of responding to pressing domestic demands. In particular, hydropower, agriculture, and tourism are viewed as optimal means to boost the economy. Pursuing such ambitious development goals often requires countries to harness shared water resources, with possible upstream and downstream implications for co-riparians.

A sense of a nation's rights also pervades the thinking on water management and cooperation in international waters. As a result, countries stake claims on shared waters based on their respective sense of rights. A number of factors come into play in a country's sense of its rights. Commonly held beliefs about the river flowing through one's country shape how people perceive rights, as do legacies of use and management under legal and constitutional instruments. Centuries of culture and tradition related to water also often instill values that influence the perception of rights. The use or nonuse of water could raise many questions about rights. In this context, the debate has moved away from a "unilateralist" view of water use, exemplified by the Harmon Doctrine (namely, "absolute sovereignty") of 1895 to a shared view of water use and cooperative management of water, illustrated by the 1997

International Watercourses Convention's principles of "reasonable and equitable use" and "no significant harm."[6]

External drivers. Externally, both regional and global influences may offer guidance and insights. ***Regional influences*** may include regional institutions, shared culture and ethnicity, regional geopolitics, and regional thinking on norms, concepts, and best practices in sustainable development. These influences will vary from basin to basin. For example, southern African countries have drawn on the regional dialogue promoted by the Southern African Development Community (SADC) and the series of regional protocols, including on Shared Watercourses. The SADC Protocol on Shared Watercourses (2000) has been used as a framework for specific basin level cooperation agreements within the Southern Africa region. In turn, the SADC Protocol drew inspiration from the International Watercourses Convention (1997). Similarly, the Economic Community of West African States (ECOWAS) has provided regional leadership on integrated water resources management (IWRM) in West Africa in the 1990 and 2000 decades. In contrast, the South Asian Association for Regional Cooperation (SAARC) has probably had less of an influence in the area of shared waters on South Asian political and water leaders.

Global trends may also exert influence, resulting in a rich virtual library of ideas and experience in international waters that countries and their partners contemplating cooperation can draw from. Appendix A provides a detailed discussion of such global influences.

Regional and global geopolitics provide similar stimulus for or against cooperation. The Iron Curtain was a deterrent against earlier cooperative action on the Danube by Western and Eastern Europe. The dissolution of the Soviet Union and the rapidly unfolding regional and global events presented unique challenges to newly independent Aral Sea countries, with implications for cooperation on several fronts, including in international waters. Good neighborliness added weight to the agreements over water that eventually were signed by the United States with Mexico and Canada, respectively.

Climate risks could pose opportunities and challenges for countries and nudge them toward cooperation. But the evidence for the climate risk-cooperation link is not forthright. In a recent study, De Stefano et al. (2010) looked at the relationship between basins likely to experience change in variability due to climate change and the robustness of the basin institutions' capacity for dealing with variability. The study found significant gaps in institutional capacities to deal with variability, especially in South America and Asia, gaps that will only grow through increased variability projected due to climate change.

Critical Country Considerations: Risks and Opportunities

Individual policy makers in a country making decisions about cooperation operate within the historical context of their countries, fed by a set of external and internal drivers of decision making, as described in the previous section. Before them is the possibility of a deal for cooperation with a set of benefits. At this point, these policy makers must choose, on behalf of their countries, whether or not to cooperate. How do they make this decision? They do not consider benefits alone, as there are many cases of countries not joining other riparians in negotiating a basin agreement (for example, the Nile) or only selectively participating as an observer (for example, the Mekong). It appears that objective or "paper" benefits (as projected in the many studies on regional cooperation or integration) are only the starting point. *Benefits are necessary, but they are insufficient, to induce cooperative action.*

A plausible explanation for the lapse in cooperation is that countries consider not only access to benefits but also about exposure to risk. Bilder (1981: 11) writes, "[the] decision to enter into an international agreement . . . will involve considerations of risk . . ." Countries may therefore discount benefits, based on perceived risks of engagement in cooperative solutions. The level and type of risks will likely vary depending on both the scope of the agreement and the hydropolitical context of the basin in question. One can also exaggerate a real risk or even perceive a risk that does not exist, as perception is influenced by many confounding factors, including political environment, historical experiences, personal goals, and salience of the issue at hand. In addition, policy makers may differ not only in how they *perceive* risks but also in how readily they will *discount* those risks (Bilder 1981). Nevertheless, perceived risks appear to lie at the core of decisions by countries to cooperate or not on issues of shared waters.

In addition to reduced risk, policy makers may also need to see positive political gains from cooperation, referred to here as "political opportunity." Even if risk is reduced to close to zero, it does not follow that policy makers will choose to cooperate, just as investments do not necessarily make sense as costs approach zero. One actually wants to see *positive* gains—both economic and political. In the mid 1980s, when the riparians of the Danube River came together, they faced not only the possibility of improved water quality monitoring (and subsequent improvement), but also the opportunity for the long sequestered western and eastern European countries to intensify communication, at least at the technical level. Likewise, the cooperative stance of Aral Sea riparians in the early 1990s has been attributed to their decision to seize the political opportunities for investments in environmental remediation (Weinthal 2002).

Assessing Risk

In this study, we suggest that the observed hesitation, or even resistance, of countries to cooperation can be better understood by evaluating the perceived risks to engagement. We define perceived risk for a given country as *the perception that an act of cooperation will expose the country to harm, will jeopardize something of value to the country, or will threaten the political future of individual policymakers.* Throughout this book, "risk" refers to "perceived risk" as defined here. In assessing such risk, country representatives ask questions, often as a series of "what if" reflections.

We propose five general categories of risk perceived by decision makers, identified through literature review.[7] The five risk types are briefly defined in table 1.1. For each case study, we explored if and how each of these five risks influenced the decision makers' engagement or non-engagement in cooperation. Thus, our first objective for this study was to determine the presence and importance of perceived risks as they influence cooperation over shared waters.

Table 1.1   Five Categories of Risk

Capacity and knowledge
Confidence in ability to negotiate a fair deal; having enough and the correct information and knowledge to do so.
Accountability and voice
Deliverability of benefits by the regional entity and co-riparians, often related to trust; having a say in decision making in the governing structures of the regional entity.
Sovereignty and autonomy
Ability to act in the best interest of the country without constraints; making decisions independently.
Equity and access
Fairness of (relative) benefits to country, including timing of benefits and costs and obtaining and retaining fair access to river.
Stability and support
Longevity potential of agreement; in-country support of agreement, including ratification likelihood.

Reducing Risk and Building Opportunity

If a country cannot find a way to compensate for or control these risks, it may choose not to enter into a cooperative agreement. Instead, it may either maintain the status quo or pursue its own interests to the extent possible without an agreement (LeMarquand 1977). However, if the risk is reduced or removed, the potential for cooperation may increase (Bilder 1981). Risk reduction is therefore of particular interest, especially for partners engaged with countries in the process of considering basin cooperation.

Policy makers may also need to see political opportunity before making the decision to cooperate. We define perceived political opportunity for a given country as *the perception that an act of cooperation will enhance the country's wellbeing, will augment something of value to the country, or will improve the political future of individual policymakers.*

For each case study, we analyzed the actions of countries and third parties that led to reduced risk and, consequently, enhanced cooperation. We also identified solutions when decision makers moved toward cooperation based on political opportunity. The second objective of this study was thus to identify actions and strategies that reduce risks and build opportunity, both serving to enhance cooperation.

Role of Third Parties

The World Bank has been involved in cooperation over international waters since the 1960 Indus Waters Treaty. The World Bank, United Nations (UN) agencies, and other development partners have played pivotal roles in such cooperation globally over the past several decades. Demand for their involvement has intensified in the wake of the 1997 International Watercourse Convention and global discussions around IWRM.

Accordingly, a central point of interest in this study is the question of *how* third parties can foster cooperation. Gaining a better understanding of suitable partner interventions will help ensure effective means of external support for cooperation. The third and final objective of this study was, therefore, to determine appropriate roles for third parties in assessing risk, reducing risk, and building opportunity.

A New Way of Looking at a Cooperation Decisions

We hypothesize that, for each country, the possibilities of cooperation and the discussion of benefits trigger an analysis of benefits and costs as well as a consideration of risks and opportunities. Furthermore, we hypothesize that the higher the benefits and opportunities relative to costs and risks, the greater the likelihood of sustained cooperation. Figure 1.1 illustrates how perceptions of political risks and opportunities might influence country decisions over cooperation, and how risk reduction and opportunity enhancement might change those perceptions over time. The northeast quadrant depicts the balance of costs/benefits and risks/opportunities most conducive to cooperation. Ideally, reducing risks and seizing opportunities when presented will move countries from their initial positions into the northeast quadrant.

Assumptions

Net Economic Benefits and Costs

We assume in this study that countries enter into a given dialogue or action with at least a preliminary understanding of the potential net

Figure 1.1   Framework: Risks and Opportunities to Cooperation

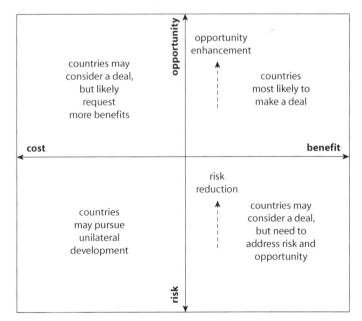

Note: Countries considering cooperation assess their positions on the x-axis in terms of net benefits (benefits less costs) and on the y-axis in terms of net opportunities (opportunities less risks). Benefits and costs are economic, while opportunities and risks are political. These "positions" in the framework may determine the likelihood of cooperation in that given situation, as described in the text in each quadrant. Risk reduction and opportunity enhancement (gray arrows) will ideally shift country positions north in the framework. Similarly, reducing economic costs and increasing economic benefits will shift countries east, which is not the focus of this particular analysis.

benefits. The prospect of cooperation is accompanied by an inventory of potential net economic benefits (x-axis). Our analysis begins at this time, when dialogue has begun and countries know what net benefits to expect. Behind this may lie several years of foundation building, including a range of basin and country analyses and consultations. Eventually, countries have a glimpse of benefits to be gained. Costs are less mentioned, but countries appear to enter into negotiations with a general calculation of how costs will reduce their net benefits.

There is considerable literature on the economic and development benefits of regional collaboration, such that the arguments in favor are practically self-evident. Benefits to cooperation (x-axis) have been emphasized in studies and discussions related to such issues as IWRM, regional integration, and regional public goods. The point of this book is not to add to this well-documented aspect, but rather to focus on other areas that are less documented. We focus on the y-axis in figure 1.1, perceived political risks and opportunities.

Cases and Tipping Points

Our starting premise is that policy leaders make specific decisions whether to cooperate over water at specific times. Thus, our focus is on a set of events for each case for which documentation and policy actors were readily accessible. We refer to the events as "tipping points," because they represent periods when policy makers in the countries involved were faced with a critical decision concerning water cooperation. We focused on tipping points in the recent past rather than the present, largely because there was a greater likelihood of documentation available compared to an ongoing cooperation deal. The use of historical events also helped avoid the risk that our analyses would impact current negotiations or controversies. Even though we did not use current events as case studies, our hope was that teams engaging with countries at the present time would use the approach proposed in this report for the design of effective strategies for their current challenges.

Five case studies were used for this analysis. For each case, we reviewed a range of documents, including available academic publications and gray literature, and scanned relevant media websites for press releases. We also conducted interviews with key decision makers wherever possible. Each case study involved an assessment of the context of the tipping point, as well as an analysis of the risks and opportunities described below that were perceived by two or three countries in each basin. For the purpose of this study, we focused on a subset of the riparians, rather than all of the countries involved in a river basin, in order to provide a detailed assessment of country perspectives. The analysis of risk perceptions was carried out for each country in line with the overall objectives of the study.

Objectives

To summarize, this book addresses the following objectives through the analysis of the five case studies:

1. Determine the presence and importance of perceived risks as they influence cooperation over shared waters.
2. Identify actions and strategies that serve to reduce risks and build opportunities.
3. Determine appropriate roles for third parties in assessing risk, reducing risk, and building opportunity.

Notes

1. According to the 1997 United Nations Convention on the Non-navigable Uses of International Watercourses, an international watercourse is a water system that flows to a common terminus, various parts of which are situated in different states. In this study, we use a variety of terms interchangeably with *international watercourse*, such as *international river basin, transboundary waters, shared waters,* and *international waters.* For the purposes of this study, all of these terms refer to rivers (surface water).
2. See, for example, Bulloch and Darwish (1993) and De Villiers (1999).
3. Giordano, Giordano, and Wolf (2005) found that the presence of an institutional mechanism for dialogue and cooperation dampens the escalation of a dispute into a full-blown conflict.
4. See, for example, Alam, Dione, and Jeffrey 2009; Yu 2008.
5. For example, see: (1) *Asia Times* (June 23, 2011): "Laos wants to pull itself out of least-developed country status by 2020"; and (2) AUCME (November 5, 2010): Ministers reaffirm "the need for Africa to foster sub-regional, regional and continental cooperation with a view to achieving sustainable development and efficient use of energy resources for the benefit of our peoples," urge "multilateral and bilateral financing institutions to create special counters and new financing mechanisms for regional dimension projects," decide to "sign a Memorandum of Understanding and Cooperation between the Conference of African Ministers in charge of Energy, the Conference of Ministers responsible for Water Resources and the Conference of Ministers of

the Environment with a view to promoting cross-border river basins development and regional electric energy production and exchange networks."

6. For more on the Convention on the Law of Non-navigable Uses of International Watercourses, see United Nations (1997).

7. See for example, Alam, Dione, and Jeffrey 2009; Bernauer and Kalbhenn 2010; Birch, Rasheed, and Drabu 2006; Browder 2000; Elhance 1999; Fischhendler and Feitelson 2003; Henwood and Funke, 2002; Linnerooth 1990; Lowi 1993; Trevin and Day 1990; and Turton 2003.

References

Alam, U., O. Dione, and P. Jeffrey. 2009. "The Benefit-Sharing Principle: Implementing Sovereignty Bargains on Water." *Political Geography* 28 (2): 90–100.

Bernauer, T., and A. Kalbhenn. 2010. "The Politics of International Freshwater Resources." In *The International Studies Encyclopedia*, ed. Robert A. Denemark. Washington, DC: International Studies Association.

Bilder, R. B. 1981. *Managing the Risks of International Agreement.* Madison, WI: University of Wisconsin Press.

Birch, D., A. Rasheed, and I. Drabu. 2006. "Sharing Waters: Engineering the Indus Water Treaty." *Civil Engineering* 159: 31–38.

Browder, G. 2000. "An Analysis of the Negotiations for the 1995 Mekong Agreement." *International Negotiation* 5: 237–61.

Bullock, J., and A. Darwish. 1993. *Water Wars: Coming Conflicts in the Middle East.* London: St. Dedmundsbury Press.

De Stefano, L., J. Duncan, S. Dinar, K. Stahl, and A. Wolf. 2010. "Mapping the Resilience of International River Basins to Future Climate Change–Induced Water Variability." Water Sector Board Discussion Paper Series 15, World Bank, Washington, DC.

De Villiers, M. 1999. *Water Wars: Is the World's Water Running Out?* London: Weidenfeld and Nicolson.

Elhance, A. P. 1999. *Hydropolitics in the 3rd World: Conflict and Cooperation in International River Basins.* Washington, DC: United States Institute of Peace Press.

Fischhendler I., and E. Feitelson. 2003. "Spatial Adjustment as a Mechanism for Resolving River Basin Conflicts: the US-Mexico Case." *Political Geography* 22: 557–83.

Giordano, M. F., M. A. Giordano, and A. T. Wolf. 2005. "International Resource Conflict and Mitigation." *Journal of Peace Research* 42 (1): 47–65.

Henwood, R., and N. Funke. 2002. "Managing Water in International River Basins in Southern Africa: International Relations or Foreign Policy." In *Hydropolitics in the Developing World: A Southern Africa Perspective*, ed. Anthony Turton and Ronald Henwood, 177–86. Pretoria, South Africa: African Water Issues Research Unit.

LeMarquand, D. G. 1977. *International Rivers: The Politics of Cooperation.* Vancouver: Westwater Research Center.

Linnerooth, J. 1990. "The Danube River Basin: Negotiating Settlements to Transboundary Environmental Issues." *Natural Resources Journal* 30: 629–60.

Lowi, M. R. 1993. "Rivers of Conflict, Rivers of Peace." *Journal of International Affairs* 49 (1): 123–44.

TFDD (Transboundary Freshwater Dispute Database). 2011. http://www.trans boundarywaters.orst.edu.

Trevin, J. O., and J. C. Day. 1990. "Risk Perception in International River Basin Management: The Plata Basin Example." *Natural Resources Journal* 30: 87–105.

Turton, A. R. 2003. "The Hydropolitical Dynamics of Cooperation in Southern Africa: A Strategic Perspective on Institutional Development in International River Basins." In *Transboundary Rivers, Sovereignty and Development: Hydropolitical Drivers in the Okavango River Basin*, ed. Anthony Turton, Peter Ashton, and Eugene Cloete, 83–103. Pretoria, South Africa: African Water Issues Research Unit and Green Cross International.

United Nations. 1997. Convention on the Law of the Non-navigational Uses of International Watercourses. UN General Assembly Resolution 51/229.

Weinthal E. 2002. *State Making and Environmental Cooperation: Linking Domestic and International Politics in Central Asia.* Cambridge, Mass.: MIT Press.

World Bank. 1993. "Water Resources Management." Policy Paper, World Bank, Washington, DC.

———. 2003. "The Water Resources Sector Strategy: Managing and Developing Water Resources to Reduce Poverty." World Bank, Washington, DC.

———. 2010a. "Sustaining Water for All in a Changing Climate, Progress Report of the Water Resources Sector Strategy." World Bank, Washington, DC.

———. 2010b. "Deepening Regional Integration." In *Africa's Infrastructure: A Time for Transformation*, ed. Vivien Foster and Cecilia Briceño-Garmendia,143–62. Washington, DC: World Bank.

Yu, W. 2008. "Benefit Sharing in International Rivers: Findings from the Senegal River Basin, the Columbia River Basin and the Lesotho Highlands Water Project." Working Paper, Africa Region, World Bank, Washington, DC.

CHAPTER 2

Application of the Framework

Introduction of the Cases and Context

The five river basins selected for this study are the Eastern Nile, Ganges, Niger, Syr Darya, and Zambezi. Cooperation mechanisms in these river basins are at varying stages. Niger and Syr Darya have basin-wide and rather formalized regional governance institutions; Eastern Nile, Ganges, and Zambezi have more limited or informal basin-wide governance institutions. The number of riparian countries in the study basins ranges from four to 10. For the countries involved, these rivers are a source of actual or potential livelihood, growth, and well-being; they are also a source of destruction through periodic floods and droughts. Thus, the basins offer a broad range of cases to develop our understanding of cooperation.

Table 2.1 provides an overview of some of the basic geographic characteristics of each basin. It is clear that these river basins cover a substantial drainage area in the aggregate and travel extensive distances through many countries.

Each case study basin has faced—and still faces—formidable challenges related to development, politics, the environment, and climate. Cooperation has been seen as one of the vehicles that countries could employ to help them meet their respective challenges. Table 2.2 highlights some of these challenges of, and opportunities arising from, cooperation.

Table 2.1   Basin Geographies

Basin	Riparian countries	Area (km²)	Average flow	Length (km)	Population (millions)
Eastern Nile	Egypt, Arab Rep.; Eritrea; Ethiopia; South Sudan; Sudan	2, 695, 300	84 BCM (at Aswan)	1,450	152
Ganges	Bangladesh, China, India, Nepal	1, 080, 000	500 BCM (at Hardinge Bridge)	2,500	400
Niger	Benin, Burkina Faso, Cameroon, Chad, Cote d'Ivoire, Guinea, Mali, Niger, Nigeria	1, 500, 000	27 BCM (at Niamey)	4,100	100
Syr Darya	Kazakhstan, Kyrgyz Republic, Tajikistan, Uzbekistan	400, 000	37 BCM	3,019	20
Zambezi	Angola, Botswana, Malawi, Mozambique, Namibia, Tanzania, Zambia, Zimbabwe	1, 370, 000	130 BCM (at outlet)	2,700	30

Sources: World Bank internal reports; Food and Agriculture Organization 2012.
Notes: The average flow data are estimates and are meant to give an idea of the volume of water involved. The average flow estimate masks seasonal differences within the year. Differences may occur among the countries in estimates for average flow; these are to be expected in any international waters context. BCM = billion cubic meters; km = kilometer; km² = square kilometer.

Each of the basins under review has also experienced a unique trajectory of movement toward cooperation. Each has either signed a bilateral or multilateral agreement, or some or all of the countries have participated in a basin (or sub-basin) institution or program.[1]

Our interest in this study is to better understand the actors that advance or inhibit basin cooperation. However, we need to first learn why policy makers in basin countries decide to cooperate or not cooperate. Accordingly, each of our cases focuses on a specific period in the recent past, referred to as a "tipping point," when the policy makers involved faced the decision whether to participate in regional cooperation on water issues. Table 2.3 shows the cases and associated tipping points.

Analysis of Cases

The following five sections present our analysis of risk perceptions and risk reduction strategies based on the Risks and Opportunities to

Table 2.2 Characteristics of Basin Water Use and Development

Basin	Development challenges	Water issues	Major uses	Opportunities
Eastern Nile	Population growth, poverty, watershed degradation, infrastructure needs, environmental and climate management (for example, floods)	Sustainable development	Hydropower, irrigation, municipal, industrial, tourism	Hydropower, irrigation, evaporation management, sediment control
Ganges	Population growth, unemployment, management of low flow seasons, surface and groundwater management	Floods, environmental degradation, water pollution, declining fisheries	Municipal, industrial, irrigation, social and cultural	Irrigation, flood management, hydropower, navigation
Niger	Poverty, population growth, urbanization and other land-use changes, low level of technical capacity	Scarcity, climate variability, floods and droughts	Agriculture (irrigation and livestock), navigation	Irrigation, hydropower, navigation
Syr Darya	Institutional difficulties (collapse of former Soviet Union)	Reduced flows due to heavy development, flooding,	Irrigation, hydropower, municipal, industrial	Hydropower, environmental flows
Zambezi	Poverty, low capacity	Floods, droughts	Municipal, industrial, irrigation, hydropower	Irrigation, hydropower, wetlands, tourism, transport

Sources: World Bank internal reports.

Table 2.3   Selected Countries and Tipping Points

Basin	Selected countries	Time period	Tipping point(s)
Eastern Nile	Egypt, Arab Rep., and Ethiopia	1999–2004	Launch of the Eastern Nile Subsidiary Action Program (ENSAP)
Ganges	Bangladesh and India	1994–98	Signing of the Ganges Water Sharing Treaty
Niger	Mali, Niger, and Nigeria	1998–2004	Revitalization of the Niger Basin Authority (NBA), originally established in 1980
Syr Darya	Kyrgyz Republic and Uzbekistan	1996–2002	Signing of the Framework Agreement on Water and Energy
Zambezi	Botswana, Mozambique, and Zambia	2000–04	Signing of the Zambezi Watercourse Commission Agreement (ZAMCOM)

Cooperation Framework. For each case, we provide a brief background that includes a description of historical context and the tipping point, followed by a discussion of the risks, opportunities, and strategies employed to move the countries toward cooperation. We focus on the perspectives of two or three of the basin countries in the context of the cooperation offer.

In these cases, the participating countries did not explicitly record perceptions of risks at the time of decision making. We inferred the perceptions from documents and discussions to which we had access. We had to rely on our professional judgment to interpret a statement or decision. Wherever possible, we tried to confirm our judgment with opinions in available documents. We also consulted with the decision makers themselves where they were accessible and with experts familiar with the situation around the tipping points studied. [2]

Eastern Nile, 1999–2004[3]

Background

The Eastern Nile is a sub-basin of the Nile and includes the five riparians of the Arab Republic of Egypt, Eritrea, Ethiopia, South Sudan, and Sudan (map 2.1). Our analysis here focuses on the perspectives of Egypt and Ethiopia during the launch and first round of investments of the Eastern Nile Subsidiary Action Program (ENSAP) during 1999 and 2004.

Recent differences among countries in the Eastern Nile basin date back several decades, when Egypt and Sudan, then under the rule of a British-Egyptian Condominium, began to irrigate cotton crops. In 1929, the two countries signed the Nile Waters Agreement regarding allocation

Map 2.1   The Eastern Nile River Basin

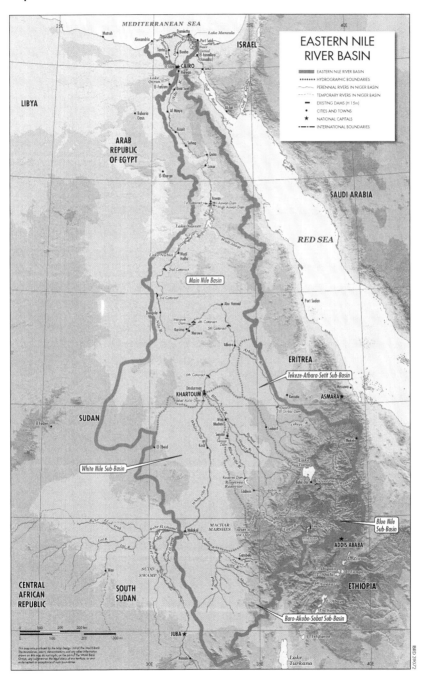

Source: World Bank, General Services Department, Map Design Unit, 2012.

of flows. Sudan erected the Sennar Dam in 1956; Egypt, eager to proceed with its plans for the Aswan High Dam, advanced the Nile Waters Treaty with Sudan in 1959. The two countries agreed to a formula for sharing the waters at Aswan, and they established a bilateral mechanism for dialogue and monitoring. Meanwhile, Ethiopia, which was not a party to this agreement, asserted its right to develop the Nile waters within its territory (Wolf and Newton 2008).

Several attempts were made by the countries and by third parties to facilitate the dialogue among all the riparians of the greater Nile basin. The Hydromet (1961), Undugu (1983), and the Tecconile (1993) initiatives were the most prominent. Some, but not all, of the riparians participated in these initiatives. In 1997, the Council of Ministers of Water Affairs of nine of the 10 riparian countries began to explore the possibility of a regional strategic plan. In 1999, the nine countries signed the minutes establishing the Nile Basin Initiative (NBI) to advance such a plan.[4] A major component of the NBI was its Subsidiary Action Programs, of which one was established for the Eastern Nile and another for the Nile Equatorial Lakes region.

The launch of the ENSAP was a major step forward for the Eastern Nile in the cooperation over water. Involving Egypt, Ethiopia, and Sudan (prior to the independence of South Sudan), its purpose was to foster development in the sub-basin, with an emphasis on investments. In 2000, the Ministers of Water Affairs approved a strategy paper. This strategy emphasized action, with a focus on investment projects that incorporated "equitable use, no significant harm and win-win solutions." Indeed, the strategy emphasized that "moving from planning to action" was key to cooperation" and "the challenge of today."

The final portfolio for the first round of the Eastern Nile investment program, called the "Integrated Development of the Eastern Nile," included a set of projects in irrigation, power interconnection, watershed management, modeling, flood preparedness, and some sub-regional studies.[5] Expected benefits to each country differed, but they were both economic and political in nature. Overall economic benefits included the potential to increase food production, energy production and access, flood and sediment management, water augmentation, and access to information and data. Overall political gains centered on the potential for establishing a platform for exchange and communication and a better mutual understanding of national development plans and their regional implications. Once agreed upon, the three countries together presented the initial portfolio of investments to donor partners in June 2001. The package included activities in a mix of water and other sectors and linked through the integrated program. Specific water allocations were not discussed, nor were they a part of this round of investments. As the projects reflected a reconciliation of the interests of the three countries, negotiations spanned a significant period of time and were quite stressful.

To advance the implementation of the ENSAP agenda, the Eastern Nile Ministers of Water Affairs jointly established the Eastern Nile Technical Regional Office (ENTRO) in 2002. Difficulties arose in defining the roles and responsibilities of this office, and in agreeing on its governance, staffing and rules of procedure. For example, country delegates to ENTRO in 2002 were unsure how to represent their countries' best interests while also making decisions beneficial to the regional organization that was to prepare and deliver projects. This issue severely constrained their action and the achievement of the key ENSAP objective of "moving from planning to action." The ministers took decisive action by closely monitoring ENSAP projects and restructuring ENTRO. By 2004, the initial difficulties were addressed and ENTRO was transformed into a fully professional institution.[6]

Analysis

Prior to 1999, both Egypt and Ethiopia saw high risks and high costs to cooperating regionally. The initial NBI process and the Eastern Nile Program offered the chance to plan together and approach global partners for funding. With mounting need for economic and social development, Ethiopia saw the possibility of accessing significant investments for the sub-basin for the first time through ENSAP. The projects it had promoted emphasized such investments in irrigation, hydropower, and watershed management. Egypt hoped for improved cooperative planning and possibilities for augmenting water supply—hence, its championing of planning models and specific river system studies in the sub-basin. The additional knowledge would allow Egypt to plan accordingly for its future. It was also an opportunity to demonstrate "good neighborliness."

When the NBI was launched in 1999 as a transitory mechanism, it was essentially an interim framework of cooperation. ENSAP was to be the forum through which the on-the-ground action occurred. Both countries approached the launch of ENSAP with some trepidation. Despite the political opportunities associated with cooperation, several risks remained. The promise of gains from cooperation was uncertain for Egypt, yet this was a new cooperative opportunity that, for the first time, included

Ethiopia. Ethiopia looked forward to significant economic benefits. Yet, the political risks inherent in opening up its development plans for outsider scrutiny remained high.

The national discourse in the countries (including views of the diaspora) was oriented to maintaining the staus quo with respect to water rights.[7] This orientation made it difficult to generate options for cooperative management of the river and to debate these options in public. The end of the series of Nile 2002 conferences did not help; the annual events had provided a platform for civil society organizations for candid debates on the future of the Nile. Moreover, both Egypt and Ethiopia also had to contend with official in-country stakeholders—ministries of foreign affairs, water, and energy—whose views had to be reconciled by the highest authorities in the respective countries. The absence of vigorous public debates and the many actors involved in national policy making presented a challenge to those engaged in the cooperative endeavors.

Both Egypt and Ethiopia appear to have moved toward cooperation in part through risk reduction measures. To start, the NBI was more of a platform than a formal agreement such as a treaty. Joining the NBI did not prejudice the countries' long-held positions with respect to water rights and water sharing. Though perceived risks differed between the countries, many of the risk reduction measures were able to target a variety of risks.

Egypt's view was that it held water rights based on historic use. Meanwhile, Ethiopia envisioned access to its share of Nile waters through Nile basin development. Provisions in ENSAP's first investment portfolio provided some assurance to both countries with respect to these risks: they both selected and prioritized short-term and medium-term projects through extensive discussions and negotiations, and included them in the first round of the investment package.

The ambiguity of ENTRO's role was a point of contention for the Eastern Nile countries. Both Egypt and Ethiopia struggled with uncertainties about the regional entity and worried about yielding sovereign national decision-making powers. Ethiopia, in particular, persistently sought clarity on the respective roles of national agencies and of ENTRO. In addition, the countries initially were skeptical about ENTRO being responsive to their national priorities and interests. These opinions took two years to work out, but eventually an elaborate system of governance was established at ENTRO, with specified rules of procedure. The countries agreed to a step-by-step decision-making process under the auspices of the ministers of water. A good line of communication had been established between the political and technical leadership of the Eastern Nile countries with periodic meetings and dialogue. The ministers also agreed that "balance" would be maintained in ENTRO's staffing to prevent dominance by one country.

While the above actions resulted from ministerial action, partners also had a role in ameliorating the situation. For example, a basin-wide program supported by donors offered capacity building and specific training to improve skills in a variety of fields related to water management and cooperation.[8] Partners worked closely with the Eastern Nile ministers by preparing "just-in-time" briefs on request and facilitated access to lessons from experiences from international river basins on request. Their commitment to extend coordinated financing for institution building, capacity development, and investments and their support for the countries' objective of using good practices in procurement, and financial and human resource management were assurances that the expectations from ENSAP were likely to be met.[9]

The risk reduction measures helped Egypt and Ethiopia in pursuing ENSAP for the first round of investments. But key risks remained. Ultimately, the countries perceived political opportunities leading to agreed decisions on ENSAP and ENTRO. Egypt had the chance to obtain a comprehensive picture of potential Nile development and project a "regional good neighbor" profile. This approach was consistent with its other moves to integrate better with Africa to expand trade, for example, as with the Common Market for Eastern and Southern Africa (COMESA). For Ethiopia, the NBI offered the opportunity to present its case to the other countries and the world, in addition to the potential to access much-needed capital and economic benefits.

Postscript

The Eastern Nile program was envisioned to foster sustainable development in the basin and to create a regional platform for cooperative dialogue and planning. ENTRO evolved into a unique and professional regional project office and was the key to the successful delivery of the first round of investments. The development of flood early warning systems, with the potential for reduced flood damage to the riparians, held promise. The countries hoped that the success of the first round of largely sectoral investments would create momentum needed to move forward on the second round of multisectoral investments. However, these additional investments have reached an impasse due to parallel political developments with respect to a formal Nile Basin treaty. The latter is still an ongoing process with clear differences among the countries. For partners, staying abreast of the changing politics in eastern Africa will help them to recognize new political opportunities. A question also remains as to whether there are stronger risk reduction measures to advance cooperation.

Ganges, 1994–98[10]

Background

The Ganges basin is shared by Bangladesh, China, India, and Nepal (map 2.2). This case study focuses specifically on the interactions between Bangladesh and India that led to their bilateral treaty on sharing of the Ganges waters at Farakka (Ganges Water Sharing Treaty) in 1996.

The tensions between India and Bangladesh over the Ganges addressed in this treaty date back as far as 1951, when Bangladesh (still part of Pakistan until 1971) learned of India's plans to construct a barrage at Farakka to divert approximately 80 percent of the Ganges dry season flow to the Hooghly River (Wolf and Newton 2008). The purpose of the barrage was to improve navigation in the port of Calcutta and to combat saltwater intrusion during the spring dry season. Although

Map 2.2   The Ganges River Basin

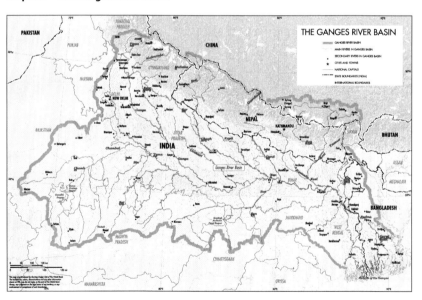

Source: World Bank, General Services Department, Map Design Unit, 2012.

the two countries engaged in dialogue on several occasions over the next two decades, they were unable to reach an agreement even as construction at Farakka began. While negotiations broke down, construction continued; in 1975, Farakka became operational. Bangladesh lodged a formal complaint against India with the United Nations a year later, which urged the parties to come to a quick settlement at the ministerial level. In 1977, India and Bangladesh signed their first bilateral Ganges agreement, valid for five years. In 1982 and 1985, they signed memoranda that extended the arrangements in the agreement until 1988 (Wolf and Newton 2008).

In the mid 1990s, following elections in both countries, new governments assumed power and the dialogue resumed. In 1996, the Ganges Treaty was signed, which served as a tipping point in the management and conflict over the Ganges for several reasons. One of the primary factors was that it was the first and only long-term agreement for the basin between India and Bangladesh, and it was also the first treaty (Salman and Uprety 2002: 170). Also important was the fact that the new governments in both countries seemed to welcome reopening negotiations in 1996 to find a conclusive outcome (Khan 1996). Until this time, both countries had persisted with their national agendas, applying a rights-based approach; by 1996, however, both countries had begun to look for mutually agreeable solutions. Although the call for cooperation was mutual, Bangladesh's new Prime Minister exerted an all-out effort to resolve the dispute with India (Salman and Uprety 2002: 170).[11] Also at this time, the state in India most reliant on the waters withdrawn at Farakka—West Bengal—expressed interest in becoming involved in the process (Hossain 1998).

The agreement under discussion included physical benefits as well as political and institutional benefits. Physically, it would restrict India's withdrawals at Farakka during the dry season from January to May, thereby guaranteeing a minimum flow to Bangladesh during this time. Flows for a variety of climatic conditions were specified in the agreement, as well as a stipulation that if conditions became drastic during the dry season and flows fell below a threshold level, the two countries must come to a new agreement. Politically, it aimed to improve overall relations between India and Bangladesh (Rahaman 2009; Salman and Uprety 2002). It included an agreement to cooperate over all shared river basins between the two countries, thus broadening the scope of cooperation over water beyond the Ganges River.

Analysis

Prior to 1996, India and Bangladesh perceived the varying cost and benefits from cooperation and also the risks associated with regional cooperation. For India, the risks were rather high, especially when compared with the expected benefits. A primary concern of India was preserving its historic use of the Ganges River: signing an agreement guaranteeing flows to Bangladesh would lock the country into a long-term commitment. To some degree, this commitment would mean a loss of authority over the water running through its territory. For Bangladesh, the risk was one of ensuring accountability for delivering benefits in terms of reliable flows in the downstream reaches of the river. Its focus was on equitable share. The country hoped to secure guaranteed minimum flows in the winter; it had repeatedly renegotiated such agreements every few years prior to the 1996 offer. Thus, for Bangladesh, the call for cooperation was largely motivated by its desire for water security. However, Bangladesh had reservations about negotiating an optimal deal with India and sustaining its implementation. In sum, the risks for Bangladesh and India were quite high at the start of the negotiations.

Eventually, both national governments were open to discussions, although neither received domestic political support initially. In India, prior to 1996, the state of West Bengal in particular was unsupportive. When West Bengal came forward with a desire to reach an agreement, this risk was somewhat reduced, but the Indian Prime Minister continued to face criticism from his constituents, who accused him of giving in to Bangladesh's demands. Similar criticism faced the Prime Minister of Bangladesh. The stability of the agreement and support for it were in doubt. Despite these uncertainties, the political leadership took a forward-looking stand in favor of cooperation.

Since Bangladesh's inherent priority was securing dry season flows, it tried to reduce this risk by proposing a trilateral agreement with Nepal as well, which could set the stage for storage further upstream. India preferred a bilateral arrangement at the time, and so the scope of the agreement was limited to India and Bangladesh. The agreement, when drafted, did provide reassurance to Bangladesh regarding its priority—it included provisions of guaranteed dry season flows, which was not the case in prior agreements.

Because of India's commitment to dry season flows, Bangladesh's expectations for economic benefits grew. India's gains were also significant since prolonging the dispute with Bangladesh would have led to the matter being raised at international forums with unpredictable pressures and results. By early 1996, with a new government in power, India began to see greater opportunity in regional cooperation; in fact, it had recently deemed it a national priority. The agreement with Bangladesh provided a chance to enhance its political image in the regional setting. Bangladesh began to view the agreement similarly and was aware of the political opportunities that could be derived from cooperating with India.

Extremely important for India was political support within the country; accordingly, the involvement of West Bengal in the process reduced the political risk. Finally, the agreement offered some predictability to India, as the process of renegotiating every few years was onerous. The involvement at the highest level by Bangladesh's prime minister also offered assurance that the agreement would be stable and predictable. For Bangladesh, risk reduction helped increase its confidence to sign the 1996 agreement. These measures centered primarily on the agreement itself, with the guarantee of dry season flows for a 30-year period. The risk of not having domestic support was not appreciably reduced prior to signing, but the national government moved forward regardless.

Opportunity enhancement measures were twofold. First, at the national level in both countries, regional cooperation was emphasized, and an agreement over the Ganges provided an opportunity to further this new mutual national goal. Second, at the regional institutional level, the agreement enhanced opportunities by including a provision for future cooperation over other basins as well as other segments of the Ganges. Both countries therefore viewed the agreement as strategic for future engagement with one another.

In early 1996, with some of the risks reduced and the opportunities apparent, Bangladesh was ready to cooperate. India, seeing many risks, also saw great political opportunities. They both signed the agreement in 1996.

Postscript

While the Ganges Water Sharing Treaty did provide a framework for future cooperation between India and Bangladesh, the agreed-upon flows to Bangladesh did not fully materialize. Several factors may be at play. First, the agreement was not comprehensive, dealing with all sources and uses. Second, it did not factor in the impacts of long-term climate change, and many analysts claim the data consulted in drafting the agreement were outdated. While the agreement stands, dissatisfaction with the treaty has been expressed periodically in both countries, and pressures on the Ganges basin continue to increase. Water-sharing agreements with quantitative allocations are inherently subject to difficulties arising from flow variations over time. Yet engagement between the parties has continued over the years, regularly building on the successes of 1996.

Niger, 1998–2004[12]

Background

The nine Niger River riparians are Benin, Burkina Faso, Cameroon, Chad, Côte d'Ivoire, Guinea, Mali, Niger, and Nigeria (see map 2.3). For this case study, we focus on the perspectives of the latter three in the context of the revitalization of the Niger Basin Authority during 1998–2004.

The Niger basin was not a site of major historical conflict over water unlike the Nile or Ganges. During colonial times, European powers used the river primarily for navigation and commerce. Following independence, in the mid-20th century, Mali and Nigeria met to define parameters for shared development of the basin; by 1961, all countries were involved in discussions. In 1963, the nine basin states signed an agreement on navigation and commerce that included principles on cooperation of the basin (Andersen et al. 2005).

In 1964, the Niger Basin Commission was established to coordinate national development among the basin states and execute a plan for integrated development. However, given several competing post-independence priorities, the commission could not demonstrate significant concrete results. The commission was converted into the Niger Basin Authority (NBA) in 1980 with the intent of bestowing on it stronger powers to advance the development of the shared Niger River. Yet again, a combination of a focus on nation building and a series of internal political and financial crises in the countries thwarted the countries' intentions in regional cooperation. Although basin-wide cooperation lagged, sub-basin agreements were finalized. These agreements included the agreement between Niger and Mali for cooperation in the utilization of the Niger River (1988), and the agreement on the shared management of border rivers between Niger and Nigeria (1990).

By 1998, the heads of state of the Niger basin and the ministers of water realized the urgent need for rapid development and the fact that NBA lacked the institutional capacity to accomplish its mission. It was clear that significant reforms were needed. At a special session of the NBA Council of Ministers, it was agreed that the council would meet regularly to discuss how to address the NBA's institutional problems while also collectively developing a plan for improving the degraded

Map 2.3 The Niger River Basin

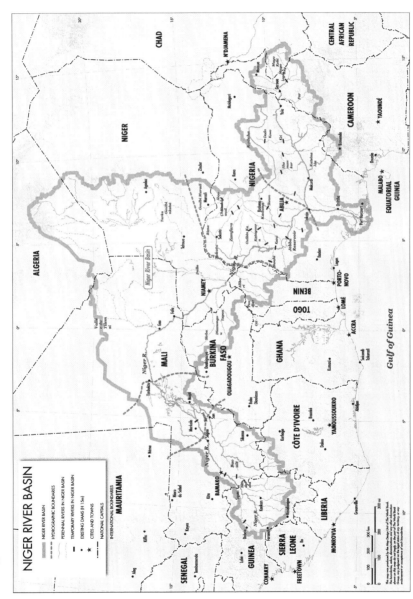

Source: World Bank, General Services Department, Map Design Unit, 2012.

environment and water resources of the basin. At the NBA's 17th ministerial session in 1998, the ministers kicked off the reform agenda and NBA entered its revitalization era. This meeting was a critical turning point in cooperation in international waters in the Niger basin. Some observers have observed that periodic meetings of leaders and heads of state of countries belonging to the Economic Community of West African States (ECOWAS) reiterating the importance of the principles of Integrated Water Resources Management and mandating member countries to implement such principles at a shared basin level had an influence on the move to revive the NBA in 1998.

In April 2004, the heads of state of the riparian countries signed the Final Communique of the Conference of Heads of State of the Niger Basin Authority and Partners, Paris (the Paris Declaration), through which they made the commitment to sustainable development and enhanced coordination and information sharing on shared waterways. The meeting in Paris was convened jointly by the then-chair of the heads of state of the basin countries and France's president and included a number of partners. The partners, in turn, signed a cooperation framework to coordinate their efforts on the Niger and align their support with NBA priorities.

The NBA subsequently pursued a fast-paced program to respond to its members' needs and interests. The renewal of regional cooperation was reflected in a new shared vision statement that the countries shaped together.[13] An institutional audit was carried out, substantial reforms were implemented, and a new management structure was put in place. The NBA then launched the preparation of the Sustainable Development Action Plan (SDAP) [14] and Investment Plan (IP) of the NBA. The SDAP was to define a strategy for the integrated and shared development process among NBA countries, while the IP was to detail the financial means. Ultimately, the SDAP and IP reflected multiple interests and were the negotiated outcomes of technical and political discussions.

Expected benefits to countries varied, but they included the following: irrigation; hydropower; environmental management, including silt control; and access to information on impacts of national activities on others. Capacity building was an integral part of the program. However, as the river had remained relatively undeveloped to this point, there were also concerns for the potential consequences of developments upstream and downstream, particularly in Mali, Niger, and Nigeria.

Analysis

Prior to 1998, Mali, Niger, and Nigeria all perceived risks associated with cooperation. Because of the relatively nonturbulent history among the riparians, their concerns about risks centered more on fears of another institutional collapse than on mutual trust; although risks were present, they were not glaringly high. The three countries also saw great political opportunities in cooperation, which is essentially why the NBA had been created decades previously. All had hopes that a successful agreement would strengthen regional alliances, enhance political images, and increase the capacity to harness development potential in the basin.

Economic development needs were a strong motivator. At the same time, the three countries were apprehensive about negotiating an acceptable program of action, given their differing needs and capacity levels. Partner support for building capacity, technical studies, and dialogue among the countries helped to advance the negotiations. Nigeria, which had the most developed infrastructure, had a keen interest in maintaining its existing flows. Its major concern was regarding upstream developments and their impacts on its water use. But Nigeria's decision makers appear to have accommodated this concern in favor of benefits to the region.

The Niger basin countries were concerned about getting their share of the benefits from cooperation to meet their development goals. There were uncertainties as to whether identified projects would be seen through to fruition—that the funding and construction of infrastructure would happen in a timely manner—since the NBA had previously failed to deliver. Clarity was needed on the flow of benefits in terms of size, timing, and sequence of benefits. The SDAP and IP had to clarify the sequence of investments proposed and estimates of funding required. In addition, the promise of a Water Charter in the near future was an assurance that rules would be adopted for the implementation of water development plans with significant regional impacts. In addition, Mali and Niger (along with other countries in the basin) needed assurances that their priorities and voices would be included within the NBA.

In sum, entering the revitalization era, all three countries saw many risks but slightly greater opportunities in committing to the NBA. Mali and Niger stood to benefit the most economically. Nigeria could expect a mix of economic and political gains; its strategy was to emphasize broader, regional economic benefits to its domestic constituents.

Risk reduction was important to all the countries, especially given the previous lack of substantive concrete action through the Niger

Basin Commission and Authority. Most of the risk reduction efforts targeted shared concerns. For example, capacity building and knowledge expansion efforts helped prepare the countries with technical skills, negotiations, and institution building. Modeling helped facilitate understanding of the complexities of the basin. Institutional reforms strengthened the confidence in NBA's accountability. The subsequent professionalization of the NBA organization contributed to the comfort of all of the countries. During the case study period (and subsequently), the two executive secretaries from Nigeria were perceived to have acted in a neutral and unbiased manner, responding effectively to the broad spectrum of interests of all the riparians. The SDAP conveyed an understanding of the three countries' priorities, and it proved to be an important communication tool as the countries approached various stakeholders with their programs.

Opportunity enhancement was also an important process in the NBA revitalization, especially for Nigeria. A significant opportunity enhancement measure on Nigeria's part was stepping into its regional leadership role, in essence looking out for regional interests rather than focusing solely on national interests. All three countries also began to see the NBA as a conduit to learn of all planned basin development—the treaty emphasized coordination among the riparians and the proposed Water Charter offered an effective tool to make it happen.

Postscript

The NBA has come a long way since the 1960s and 1980s. Following the adoption of the SDAP and IP, feasibility studies began in the basin, and a robust investment program is in place with substantial commitments from partners. National agencies in water have enhanced their capacity in basin management. The investment program, initially slow, has accelerated. The countries continue to work together and consider cooperative development as an attractive option. A Water Charter has been ratified by eight of the nine countries. The level of conflict has remained low.

The challenge remains one of fulfilling the major expectations of all of the member countries while ensuring the professional implementation of the Water Charter. In addition, new challenges from changing demographics, water use, food and energy insecurities, infrastructure development, and climate risks will emerge and could test the robustness of the cooperative arrangements.

Syr Darya, 1996–2002[15]

Background

The Syr Darya is a relatively new international basin, achieving this status in 1991 with the collapse of the former Soviet Union. There are four riparians on the Syr Darya River: Kazakhstan, Kyrgyz Republic, Tajikistan, and Uzbekistan (map 2.4). The river originates in the Kyrgyz Republic and flows through Uzbekistan and Tajikistan before returning to Uzbekistan. Eventually, it passes through the Kazakh steppe and flows into the Aral Sea. This analysis focuses on the perspectives of, and interactions between, the Kyrgyz Republic and Uzbekistan from 1996–2002.

Historically, the river has been used for irrigation and hydropower. In the 1950s, the Soviet Union embarked on a vast land reclamation program involving massive irrigation schemes, including dams and reservoirs, to increase the cotton harvest. This eventually resulted in environmental degradation—from pesticides, soil salinization, and industrial

Map 2.4   The Syr Darya River Basin

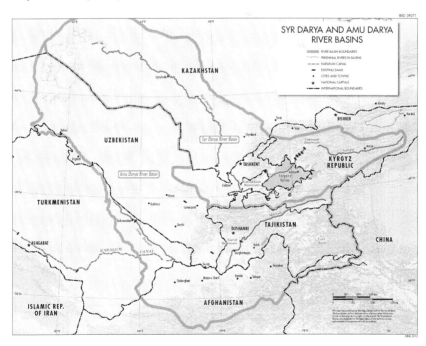

Source: World Bank, General Services Department, Map Design Unit, 2012.

waste—and depleted river flows (Wolf and Newton 2008). Water used for cotton had previously flowed into the Aral Sea, where it compensated for evaporation. When the flow into the sea was cut to a small fraction, the sea lost 80 percent of its surface area and 90 percent of its volume.

In the 1980s, the Soviet government established a centralized water management entity in Tashkent for the Syr Darya to operate and maintain large infrastructures and manage water allocations among the riparians. It coordinated the release of water from the reservoirs. At the time, the focus was on irrigation rather than hydropower. For instance, 75 percent of the water from the Toktogul reservoir, located in the upstream state that is today the Kyrgyz Republic, was released during the growing season from April to September. This benefited the downstream Soviet states (today's Uzbekistan and Kazakhstan) for their cotton cultivation. In turn, these countries were asked to send coal and gas upstream for winter heating needs. This exchange effectively took place without borders or any market mechanisms, for the primary purpose of growing cotton.

With the dissolution of the Soviet Union, these institutional mechanisms broke down. Countries began searching for sustainable solutions to meet their now-conflicting energy and agriculture needs. As they emerged into independence, the Syr Darya riparian states were confronted with the end to Moscow's funding of much of the costs of the operation and maintenance of dikes, reservoirs, and dams. Even in areas where they had technical expertise, formulating a new system of water and energy management that reflected a state rather than a regional set of priorities was daunting. Raising capital and even operating funds was a serious challenge. While the global concern over the fate of the Aral Sea brought access to donor funding in a number of areas, the aid did not usually extend to maintaining and operating the existing infrastructure, notably in the Kyrgyz Republic.

To address these issues, in early 1992, immediately after independence, the riparian states negotiated an agreement to maintain the Soviet water management system. But energy deliveries to the Kyrgyz Republic during winter were not part of the agreement. In the absence of this commitment, the Kyrgyz Republic had to rely on releases from Toktogul's water for hydropower generation in winter. A constraint was that the Naryn-Syr Darya river systems included a cascade of reservoirs dominated by Toktogul. There was little capacity for storage in the downstream countries, yet seasonal demands for irrigation had to be met.

In 1998, Kazakhstan, the Kyrgyz Republic and Uzbekistan signed the Agreement on Water and Energy, which Tajikistan joined in 1999. The agreement was for a five-year period. The United States Agency for International Development (USAID) extended extensive support to the countries to assist them in reaching the agreement. The agreement specified that the Kyrgyz Republic would release a specified flow down the river each month from the Toktogul dam, as well as supply electricity to Kazakhstan and Uzbekistan during the growing season, in exchange for gas and coal during the winter months to meet increased demand at home. The exchanges were designed as a barter system mimicking the Soviet days, with the intention of supporting a water-energy management regime that would be mutually beneficial, balancing energy and agricultural needs. The agreement provided for "future joint activities concerning rational use of water, fuel, and energy." Thus, a distinguishing feature was the linked multisectoral benefits to be gained from managing the river cooperatively. Related agreements were signed on the operation of energy systems and cooperation on environmental matters. Its implementation was to be facilitated through periodic meetings among the countries and through the use of models to optimize reservoir operations.

The agreement was formulated against the backdrop of significant institutional development at the regional scale in the Aral Sea basin. Since the early 1990s, the riparian countries of the Amu Darya and Syr Darya River Basins had established and endorsed a network of institutional mechanisms for coordinating their water management activities and mobilizing resources to fight the problem of a much-depleted and receding Aral Sea. The inventory of institutional mechanisms is long. The Aral Sea countries seized several opportunities to state their interest in regional cooperation and work together to solve common problems. However, there were considerable differences among them on effective water resources management under the new circumstances they found themselves in the post–Soviet Union period.

Analysis

In 1998, all of the post–Soviet rule countries were still in a period of transition, having recently regained independent statehood. Despite the risks in a cooperative arrangement, the Kyrgyz Republic and Uzbekistan saw greater benefits than costs in a regional perspective, even though the alternative of unilateral action allowed for greater autonomy in decision making. For example, if the Kyrgyz Republic would operate Toktogul reservoir in an irrigation mode, Uzbekistan and Kazakhstan would meet their irrigation needs in the growing season. In return, if Uzbekistan and Kazakhstan were to commit to winter energy deliveries to the Kyrgyz Republic, all the parties would benefit. The Kyrgyz Republic would experience gains despite the loss of some autonomy in decisions regarding water releases. The alternative would be for the Kyrgyz Republic to retain complete control of the Syr Darya's flows year round. Then it would not have to seek out alternative energy sources in the winter or rely on its neighbors to supply the energy. However, in this situation, it would have to bear all of the costs of operating the hydroelectric infrastructure. Uzbekistan would have to deal with decisions on water management in winter to deal with excess flows.

Hydropower generation in the winter posed concerns for Uzbekistan. In addressing this concern through the cooperative arrangement, the Kyrgyz Republic faced another challenge—funding the operation and maintenance of the substantial infrastructure of dams, canals, and other equipment in the absence of the Soviet structure. There was no precedent of charging downstream riparians for the operation and maintenance of upstream infrastructure. Not only was the Kyrgyz Republic concerned about relying on other countries for its critical seasonal fuel needs, but also there was the additional worry that the agreement would mean a loss of autonomy to pursue its own energy needs and priorities for the sake of other sectoral priorities downstream. Uzbekistan was motivated by its own economic development, which was dependent on the cotton irrigation scheme in the Ferghana valley, a major foreign exchange earner. Thus, its preference clearly was for adequate supply of irrigation water in the spring and summer. Upstream decisions on hydropower were problematic for the autonomous development of the country's commercial strengths.

One explanation for the forward momentum on the 1998 agreement was the feeling that political opportunity would be enhanced, even though critical risks remained. Regional cooperation after the fall of the Soviet Union was part of the national policies of many of the new states, including the Kyrgyz Republic and Uzbekistan. International agencies, who sought to support the emergence of a strong and stable Central Asia, were willing to facilitate activities and agreements related to regional cooperation, and the 1998 agreement was a step in that direction. In addition, as the countries made the transition to independence, they were conscious of enhancing their political image and profile outside the region, and they considered demonstrating their willingness to respond to regional needs to be a favorable move. Such demonstrations also helped to generate much-needed external funding from international financing institutions, the United Nations, and bilateral donors (Weinthal 2002).

To address issues of integrated planning and management of water and energy systems, the USAID offered assistance for the modeling of the basin and the application of hydromet systems, which helped the countries better understand both hydrology and policy implications of various operating rules. For some time, these models helped to review and revise coordinated reservoir operations. However, an alternative to the barter system for water and energy was not agreed upon, so concerns over equity in benefits for the most part remained on both sides. The agreement did, however, include language on cost-sharing for the Kyrgyz Republic for infrastructure operations. Kazakhstan, the Kyrgyz Republic, and Uzbekistan signed the agreement in 1998 despite the risks.

The agreement was meant to secure water and energy to meet the needs of the four riparian states. Unfortunately, the Framework Agreement was only temporarily successful in this regard. Changing politics, economic contexts, and the re-emergence of risk perceptions that had played a major part in the signing of the agreement also led to its eventual collapse. There were difficulties in the agreement: the energy-for-energy exchange assumed a level of pricing of hydro energy and fossil fuel energy that did not work out in practice, given market fluctuations of prices (Bernauer and Siegfried 2006). The emergence of private sector players in the energy sector was a deterrent to maintaining commitments on pricing, given attractive world prices.

Postscript

Ultimately, both Kazakhstan and Uzbekistan failed to deliver the agreed-upon water and energy flows for several years, and the Kyrgyz Republic did not always release the stipulated volumes of water. Uzbekistan sought greater autonomy to manage its spring and summer needs through alternative sources. Meanwhile, political turbulence marked the 2000 decade in the Kyrgyz Republic. Relations among the countries affected cooperative activities. Thus, the political opportunity available in the mid 1990s, namely, better overall relations among the former Soviet states and a willingness to explore options for regional cooperation, no longer existed in 2002–03. Also, despite the risk reduction measures deployed through the 1998 agreement, the earlier risks resurfaced. Over time, the countries were not convinced of the continuing political gains to keep the agreement alive.

Zambezi, 2000–04[16]

Background

The Zambezi basin is shared among eight riparians: Angola, Botswana, Malawi, Mozambique, Namibia, Tanzania, Zambia, and Zimbabwe (map 2.5). This assessment centers on the perspectives of Botswana, Mozambique, and Zambia.

Efforts at cooperative management in the Zambezi basin—beyond the scope of navigation—essentially began with interest in constructing the Kariba dam. In 1955, a bilateral power board was established between Northern and Southern Rhodesia, now Zambia and Zimbabwe. This board in 1958 oversaw the construction of the dam on the main stem of the Zambezi River between Zambia and Zimbabwe.

Shortly after Zambia and Zimbabwe gained independence (in 1967 and 1980, respectively), the two countries signed the Zambezi River Authority Agreement, creating an institutional structure (replacing the former power board) to develop and utilize the Zambezi's waters in ways that were beneficial to the two countries. At the same time, the United

Map 2.5   The Zambezi River Basin

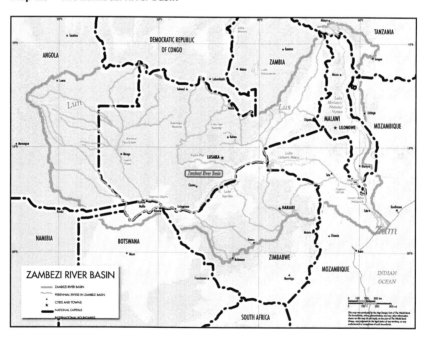

Source: World Bank, General Services Department, Map Design Unit, 2012.

Nations Environment Programme (UNEP) launched a water management program in Africa, selecting the Zambezi for one of its projects—the Zambezi River Action Plan, which received initial support from environmental agencies in Botswana, Zambia, and Zimbabwe. This plan was intended to coordinate sustainable development to prevent future conflicts, but it did not advance.

There was another attempt during the mid 1980s to act on the Zambezi River Action Plan, but the process was stalled. However, discussions regarding some of the associated projects were successful in creating a multilateral forum. Through this forum, many of the riparians proposed developing a regional agreement to provide an enabling environment for cooperative development on the Zambezi. In 2000, the revised Southern African Development Community's (SADC) Protocol on Shared Watercourses provided a model for the Zambezi as well as other shared watercourses.[17]

After the adoption of the SADC Protocol, discussions in the Zambezi basin refocused on developing a basin-wide agreement. For several years, the Zambezi countries pursued an agreement, supported by a donor-funded program that included other capacity-building activities and studies. A secretariat established in Lusaka coordinated these basin-wide efforts; all the basin states except Zambia signed the Agreement on the Establishment of the Zambezi Watercourse Commission (ZAMCOM) in 2004. The riparian countries, motivated by the recent economic recovery, were eager to pursue new development projects. They also viewed a basin-wide agreement as an instrument for strengthening political ties and attracting investments and donor support. In addition, they shared a growing sense that the unilateral development that characterized the status quo had its limitations in terms of managing the river's many challenges.

Though the benefits of cooperation were clearly articulated, they remained elusive in practice, because the countries had varying expectations of, and likely perceived a range of, differing risks and opportunities in signing the ZAMCOM Agreement. On the one hand, some of the riparians saw the potential for a better understanding of other countries' actions on the Zambezi, and also the potential for securing their water supply, improving flood management, developing hydropower and irrigation, and increasing water transport potential. They also expected access to new funding. On the other hand, the countries had concerns about the possible erosion of autonomy in decision making at the national level. The concerns of the riparians reflected the different principled positions, from those that favored unilateral development to those that desired a community of co-riparian states. Perceived capacity and knowledge constraints also held some countries back from concluding any basin-wide agreements for fear of ending up with an inequitable share of the benefits.

Analysis

The risk situation in the Zambezi highlighted the concerns around the autonomy to undertake development programs and equity to access the expected share of benefits under cooperative river management. Countries had to contend with internal discussions about these risks with domestic stakeholders in a context where there were no firm guarantees about projected benefits. Moreover, other water cooperation deals in the basin were a mix of positive and negative experiences. This legacy of past agreements colored the views toward the proposed ZAMCOM Agreement and what it would entail for benefit and cost flows.

Zambia saw high risks and low benefits in committing to ZAMCOM, while Botswana and Mozambique saw high benefits and indeed risks in *not* engaging in cooperative efforts to access opportunities. This difference in perceptions is partly due to the varying dependencies of the countries on the basin for water supplies. The majority of the Zambian population (90 percent) was located in the basin, and its area was about 42 percent of the total basin area. In contrast, 16 percent of the population of Mozambique and 1 percent of the population of Botswana resided in the basin. Zambia contributed over 40 percent of the mean annual run-off, compared to an estimated 1.2 percent by Botswana and 11 percent by Mozambique.

Zambia, driven by large-scale economic development needs, sought capital to pursue such development.[18] In theory, a ZAMCOM-type agreement could be beneficial. However, the agreement offered in 2004 was not accompanied by an investment program with financing commitments. In the absence of a clear and well-sequenced investment program, Zambia's short-term gains were uncertain. However, there could be several risks, including perceived roadblocks to the implementation of its development plans.

Zambia presented several reasons for its reluctance based on its view that it may be disadvantaged because of relatively lower negotiation capacities. These included an outdated water law from 1949 that included specific provisions excluding parts of the Zambezi River; the absence of a water policy that dealt with transboundary matters; and inadequate internal consultation with civil society. At the same time, concerns about autonomy and uncertainties about obtaining an equitable share of the benefits from cooperation were significant hurdles.

Mozambique and Botswana also faced risks. Mozambique had concerns related to its significant dependence on shared international waters. The majority of Mozambique's waters originated in, and traveled through, other countries.[19] Thus, knowledge about basin development and riparian activities was critical for its own development plans as well as for action with respect to water and flood management.[20] Botswana, too, was heavily dependent on international rivers, and noncooperation could impose a high cost on its own development plans.[21]

Mozambique's concerns about basin-wide developments would be addressed through the information-sharing provisions of the agreement and the platform it offered for sharing plans and programs. The Zambezi Commission would also provide a potential forum to motivate cooperative action on recurring flood problems and for forcefully presenting its case to the outside world for environmental flows to maintain a healthy delta.

Postscript

To date, Zambia remains the only country in the Zambezi basin that has not signed the agreement. Seven others have signed it, and six have ratified it. The agreement became effective in June 2011. Meanwhile, it is likely that the Zambezi countries will want to accelerate implementation of their ambitious development plans, making regional cooperation even more critical. Climate change impacts would bring additional challenges to a fragile situation. As an observer of ZAMCOM, Zambia would have access to basin-wide information. Ultimately, Zambia would have to see a clear flow of benefits, including a sequence of investments, and its perceived risks to autonomous development would have to be reduced. The Niger Basin's Sustainable Development Action Plan and the related Investment Program might provide useful pointers in this direction. Much also depends on the evolving regional politics in southern Africa, with the end of major civil conflicts and accelerated economic growth and the emergence of new political alignments. The question will be whether the emerging political scenario will open up new opportunities for cooperation in international waters.

Summary

A few observations are worth highlighting at this point. First, although each case was unique, many showed similarities in perceived risks. An in-depth discussion of the risks as they emerged in our analysis follows in chapter 3. Second, it is clear from our five case studies that risk reduction

Figure 2.1 Summary of Key Observations

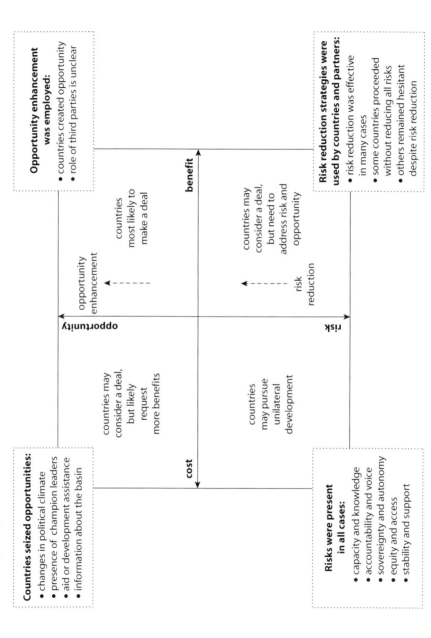

Notes: Key observations are from the five case studies as related to identifying risks, identifying risk reduction strategies (and the role of third parties), and identifying how to anticipate and seize opportunity. These observations are expanded upon in the following chapters.

50

was important in moving countries toward cooperation. As for many countries, some risks either remain or have reemerged, resulting in stagnancy or regression. A discussion and grouping of risk reduction strategies that were effective in our case studies is presented in chapter 4. Third, the role of partners varied greatly among our cases—some countries took the initiative for risk reduction, while others benefited from outside assistance. Chapter 5 offers recommendations for partners based on these cases, including ways of using risk-appropriate intervention strategies for reducing risk, and laying the groundwork for seizing political opportunity. Finally, the cases present varying degrees of "successful" cooperation. It appears agreements are rather dynamic, which raises several important questions for partners, also discussed in the chapters that follow. Figure 2.1 illustrates some of these notable observations.

Notes

1. The most up-to date agreements pertaining to cooperation for the study basins can be found by searching the Transboundary Freshwater Dispute Database (TFDD) (2011), http://www.transboundarywaters.orst.edu/database/interfreshtreatdata.html.

2. Attribution is difficult given the political sensitivities around the issues of cooperation decisions.

3. The Eastern Nile section was prepared in collaboration with Barbara Miller, Eileen Burke, and J.B. Collier.

4. The 10 original riparians were Burundi, Democratic Republic of Congo, Egypt, Ethiopia, Eritrea, Kenya, Rwanda, Sudan, Tanzania, and Uganda. Eritrea opted to participate in the NBI as an observer. Today, there are 11 riparian countries in the Nile basin with the inauguration of South Sudan as a new country in July 2011.

5. The investment program included seven sub-projects: Eastern Nile Planning Model; Baro-Akobo sub-basin and Multi-Purpose Water Resources Development; flood preparedness and early warning; irrigation and drainage development; watershed management; and hydropower development and regional power trade, including Ethiopia-Sudan Transmission Interconnection and the Eastern Nile Regional Power Trade Study. Of these, the Eastern Nile Planning Model; flood preparedness and early warning; the first round of irrigation investments; Ethiopia-Sudan Transmission Interconnection; and watershed management projects were to be fast-tracked. The ministers agreed that the fast track projects were to be included for presentation to donors for immediate support, while the other three projects, largely of a study and program identification nature were to be considered for longer-term

development: regional power trade; regional irrigation and drainage; the Baro-Akobo sub-basin and Multi-Purpose Water Resources Development.

6. A competitively recruited chief executive from the region in 2004 was evidence of the move to professionalization. Political interests were critical but were managed by the respective ministers and heads of state alongside the renewal of ENTRO.

7. Various media reports.

8. The basin-wide Shared Vision Program of the NBI was a US$130 million initiative covering key water-related sectors to build capacity and confidence.

9. The first round of ENSAP-related investments of approximately US$300 million occurred in 2006–07.

10. The Ganges section was prepared in collaboration with Brendan Galipeau, Claudia Sadoff, and Aaron Wolf.

11. Seventy-six percent of Bangladesh's population resides in the Ganges basin.

12. The Niger section was prepared in collaboration with Aminou Tassiou, Audace Ndayizeye, J. B. Collier, and Amal Talbi.

13. In May 2005, the extraordinary session of the NBA Council of Ministers held in Abuja adopted the shared vision statement, which states that the Niger basin is "a common space of sustainable development through an integrated management of water resources and related eco-systems, for the enhancement of the living conditions and prosperity of the populations by 2025."

14. The SDAP sets out the basin's regional priorities based on these priority domains: conservation of the ecosystems, development of socioeconomic infrastructures, and capacity building for the stakeholders.

15. The Syr Darya section has been prepared in collaboration with Daryl Fields, Simon Croxton, Martha Jarosewich-Holder, Alfred Diebold, and Frank Schrader.

16. The Zambezi section was prepared in collaboration with Marcus Wishart, Thomas Bernauer, and Lucas Beck.

17. The Orange–Senqu (2000) and Limpopo (2003) basin agreements followed the SADC Protocol (2000).

18. See World Bank (2009), Zambia Country Water Resources Assistance Strategy.

19. Mozambique is downstream of nine international rivers.

20. Floods were an annual occurrence costing about 1.5 percent of national gross domestic product. See World Bank (2009), *Zambia—Managing Water for Sustainable Growth and Poverty Reduction: Country Water Resources Management Assistance Strategy*. Also see World Bank (2010).

21. An excerpt from the State of the Nation address by the president of Botswana, November 2011: "Government remains committed to drawing some 495 million cubic meters of water per annum from the Chobe-Zambezi River system, for medium and long term development. In line with this requirement, final notes to SADC and Member States have been sent in accordance with the revised SADC Protocol on Shared Watercourses."

References

Andersen I., O. Dione, M., Jarosewich-Holder, and J. Olivry. 2005. *The Niger River Basin: A Vision for Sustainable Management: Directions in Development.* Washington, DC: World Bank.

Bernauer, T., and T. Siegfried. 2006. "Estimating the Performance of International Regulatory Regimes: Methodology and Empirical Application to International Water Management in the Naryn Syr Darya Basin." *Water Resources Research* 43: 1–14.

Hossain, I. 1998. "Bangladesh-India Relations: the Ganges Water Sharing Treaty and Beyond." *Asian Affairs: An American Review* 25 (3): 131–50.

Khama, I. 2011. State of the Union Address. Botswana, November.

Rahaman, M. M. 2009. "Principles of Transboundary Water Resources Management and Ganges Treaties: An Analysis." *Water Resources Development* 25 (1): 159–73.

Salman, M. A., and K. Uprety. 2002. *Conflict and Cooperation on South Asia's International Rivers.* Washington, DC: World Bank.

TFDD (Transboundary Freshwater Dispute Database). 2011. http://www.transboundarywaters.orst.edu.

FAO (Food and Agriculture Organization). 2012. Aquastat. http://www.fao.org/nr/water/aquastat/main/index.stm.

Weinthal, E. 2002. *State Making and Environmental Cooperation: Linking Domestic and International Politics in Central Asia.* Cambridge, Mass.: MIT Press.

Wolf, A. T., and J. T. Newton. 2008. "Cases of Transboundary Dispute Resolution. Appendix C." In *Managing and Transforming Water Conflicts*, ed. J. Delli Priscoli and A. T. Wolf, 169–248. New York: Cambridge University Press.

World Bank. 2009. *Zambia: Managing Water for Sustainable Growth and Poverty Reduction: A Country Water Resources Assistance Strategy.* World Bank Water Resources Management Africa Region. Washington, DC: World Bank.

———. 2010. *The Zambezi River Basin: A Multi-Sector Investment Opportunities Analysis.* Vol. 1–4. Washington, DC: World Bank.

CHAPTER 3

Understanding Risk

The analysis in chapter 2 leads to a discussion about political risks involved in international cooperation—or the lack of international cooperation—over water. According to our analytical framework, these risks factor into countries' and leaders' decisions whether to cooperate. In this chapter, we discuss how the five categories of risk—the y-axis in the analytical framework—weigh into the cooperation decision.

The Five Categories of Risk

This chapter begins with a discussion of how we identified perceived risks in the five case studies. The five categories of risk introduced in chapter 1 are capacity and knowledge, accountability and voice, sovereignty and autonomy, equity and access, and stability and support. These risks are discussed in detail in following sections, using examples from the case studies.

Capacity and Knowledge

This risk refers to a country's confidence in its capacity—skills or expertise—to negotiate an agreement and to a country's sufficient technical knowledge (for example, of basin hydrology) to do so. Policy makers, who may believe that they do not have as much capacity as their negotiating partners, may have apprehensions about being in a weak bargaining position. Ethiopia and several of the Equatorial Nile countries have consistently requested help to upgrade their transboundary departments and basin analysis skills, for example, in modeling.[1] In the Niger basin, preparation of the Sustainable Development Action Plan (SDAP) provided the countries with the opportunity to access up-to-date development scenarios to plan their water program. Many of the Niger basin countries had faced decades of internal crises and needed to upgrade their skills and capacities in integrated water resources management (IWRM) in line with their national policies. Zambia, which had always expressed concern about its capacity in transboundary matters, had requested assistance with building skills in international waters and negotiations.

Significant gaps may exist in knowledge and information about basin hydrology, ecology, markets, and economics. For example, if available master plans do not reflect current realities in terms of basin water supply and demand, or if the likely effects of climate variability and change have not been investigated, countries may feel they are not entering negotiations well equipped to make a deal. Going to the negotiating table with dated information could be a challenge for the riparian countries.[2] Countries then may not be able to raise pertinent questions about the projections of costs and benefits. Such a situation may hinder the understanding of the various unilateral and cooperative development options, leaving countries uncertain as to whether they had all the options available.

All of the basins studied faced this challenge. In the Ganges basin, the countries depended on old data to shape their final agreement. Likewise, the Eastern Nile countries had apprehensions about the adequacy of their knowledge of Eastern Nile river systems. The Arab Republic of Egypt wanted a better understanding of upstream hydrology. Ethiopia wanted a rapid update of the dated basin studies. Uzbekistan and the Kyrgyz Republic, still in the early stages of state building, were unsure of devising appropriate and effective economic schemes for water and energy management in the 1990s to replace the former Soviet system and of making them work. In the absence of reliable and accurate information, some long-held myths about water availability and water control may persist. Such myths, in turn, may reinforce the perceived risks of cooperation and the benefits of unilateralism.

The capacity and knowledge risk is linked to the sovereignty and autonomy risk. "Without knowledge, riparian states are extremely nervous about threats to sovereignty, especially when another riparian is deemed to have that knowledge and is therefore 'powerful'" (GFID 1998: 13). It also affects a country's concerns for equity, as it may lead a country to fear that it would not be capable of negotiating a "fair" deal.

Accountability and Voice

This risk refers to a country's concerns about the answerability of other parties regarding the delivery of benefits as offered in a deal. The concerns usually stem from a lack of confidence in the intent or ability of co-riparians or third parties to deliver on such commitments. The concern extends also to skepticism about the ability of regional mechanisms, such as river basin entities established by the participating countries. In the Syr Darya, countries did not seem confident that the commitments of water and energy exchange would be met. The formation of the Eastern Nile Office was beset by anxieties in the participating countries that it would not deliver what each one of them wanted and that it would not adequately respond to their priorities. Similarly, in the Niger River basin, the riparians worried about the accountability of the Niger Basin Authority to deliver the fruits of cooperation.

The risk type also includes a country's perception that it may not be adequately heard and included in the decision-making processes at the regional level. Countries in our case samples were concerned that the governance arrangements of the regional entity would not allow for adequate and inclusive levels and systems of decision making, approval, monitoring, dispute settlement, and enforcement of commitments. These concerns related to political (ministerial level) decision making, technical advisory arrangements, and technical review and monitoring mechanisms. This concern was acute in the early years of the Eastern Nile program. Also, countries expected to play "equal" roles in any regional mechanism and did not want to be overwhelmed by the more powerful countries. In addition, countries saw the regional forum as a platform for presenting their particular case and context (for example, needs or rights) to other riparians and obtain responsive solutions.

In short, country concerns were related to governance, decision-making structures and processes, and rules of engagement. Agreed approval processes, decision-making steps, and operating procedures were critical elements of a regional cooperative organization to build confidence among participating countries. In some cases, there were concerns about balance among countries in the staffing and leadership of the regional entity. In a joint institution, dominance by any one country was not acceptable. Finding qualified personnel from all the participating countries was highly valued. Both the Eastern Nile and the Niger basins had a strong sentiment to ensure the presence of participating country professionals in the regional office and projects. The professionalization occurred over time, and it was preceded by a period when staff played representational roles, carrying the burden of their respective country's formal positions on water development and management, even as they made decisions in the regional office—decisions demanding a regional rather than a national hat.

Countries also saw participation in regional forums as a way of presenting their views to the outside world, thereby gaining appreciation and recognition of their predicaments. The Syr Darya basin countries were successful in this regard, using regional forums to present their post-Soviet context and environmental challenges, and attracting attention and funding to their many development needs. Many felt that the Nile 2002 conferences (1992–2002) provided a platform for a variety of governmental and nongovernmental voices from the riparian countries to be heard, and they allowed for the articulation of views that defended and criticized the status quo. In the case of the Ganges, India felt it had the chance to refurbish its overall foreign policy image by reaching out to Bangladesh (Rahaman 2009; Salman and Uprety 2002).

Sovereignty and Autonomy

This risk refers to a country's desire to have control over resources and infrastructure and to make decisions independently. At its core, this risk is about countries sensing the danger of intrusive external management of sovereign decision-making prerogatives. All of the cases reflect this risk perception, to varying degrees. In the Zambezi, Zambia has been worried about ceding control over much-needed national development decisions. During the early years of the Eastern Nile Office, there were long and persistent debates on "national" and "regional" responsibilities following countries' concerns that the long hand of regional institutions would extend into the decisions of national agencies.

Globally, the paradigm shift from a unilateral "absolute sovereignty" approach to accommodating the principles of "reasonable and equitable utilization and avoidance of significant harm"[3] has been a slow and gradual process. Similarly, countries may start with fairly narrow mandates for the regional organization at the basin level when trust is low and sovereignty concerns are acute. With increased confidence and trust, they may widen these mandates and related powers to permit a broader scope of action by the regional entity. The cases reflect this dilemma facing the countries—they participated in regional arrangements to pursue development goals through cooperation as opportunities opened up, yet they resisted any perceived attempt to direct decision making or supervise implementation at the national level. The countries' political leadership periodically reviewed the mandates and powers of the cooperative regional entities they had set up to ensure that the boundaries of responsibilities and accountabilities clearly reflected principles of sovereignty and subsidiarity.

The sovereignty risk comes across as one of the two (the other being the equity risk) deeply felt concerns for a country contemplating cooperation. At its core is a mix of cultural, political, and values-based perceptions of the need to own, manage, and control one's future. "Selling the country up (or down) the river" is a particularly apt phrase that defines the fears in cooperative deals. Countries in our case mix had to periodically deal with this risk perception throughout the period of the study. The perception may be temporarily abated through risk reduction measures, but the countries might continue to engage one another while carrying this deep-seated worry.[4]

Equity and Access

This risk refers to countries' concerns for fairness in the agreement—whether it is in specified quantity or quality of water, benefit flows, or project costs—as well as its sense of entitlement to use its fair share of the river. Who gets benefits now and who has not received benefits to date are critical questions. Ethiopia was very concerned about unlocking the potential for Nile basin development as early as possible from regional cooperation. Zambia was worried that Zambezi cooperation would inhibit its internal development, despite the fact that Zambia occupies a major part of the basin. Niger and Mali sought investments to address major poverty and growth constraints, and regional cooperation was a means to that end.

In addition to accessing potential benefits was the larger question of equitable rights. The many debates around legal and environmental principles in the mid-1990s have not yet specified the bases for estimating such rights.[5] Countries define "equitable rights" as they see it, in the absence of a precise, agreed-upon set of criteria. For some, it is maintaining what they perceive as an existing right. India and Egypt both saw equity as continuing with their historic uses of the rivers. Likewise, Uzbekistan's insistence to maintain flows for cotton irrigation related to its notion of equity. However, Bangladesh wanted to secure dry season flows. Ethiopia was keen to develop Nile waters to address serious food and energy security challenges. The Kyrgyz Republic sought to serve its winter energy interests. Niger felt a great sense of urgency to use the Niger River for immediate development needs. Zambia considered Zambezi cooperation to be fair only if it could pursue its much needed development goals.

The notion of "equity" in our cases extended beyond sharing water to sharing benefits as well as the timing of benefits. The Kyrgyz Republic needed energy resources only in winter; Uzbekistan needed river flows during the spring and summer growing seasons. Inequities were seen not only in terms of the quantity of benefits but also in the timing of their delivery. India and Bangladesh debated at length as to the quantity and timing of the Ganges water to be shared. In all of these cases, countries paid considerable attention to analyzing expected benefit flows and assessing related risks. Given the lack of precise criteria for equity, decisions regarding water and benefit sharing appear to be negotiated based on both economic and political criteria.

Stability and Support

This risk refers to a country's concern that an agreement would not be welcomed by its own citizens nor widely supported politically within the country. It applies not only to the implementability of an agreement, but also to a decision-maker's positive or negative public image and re-election potential. The constituents of India and Bangladesh criticized their respective leaders for deciding on an agreement. Part of Zambia's stated reluctance to sign the Zambezi agreement was lack of domestic support. Zambia also stated that its current water legislation did not support regional agreements. The evolution of cooperation on the Danube River in the 1980s and 1990s vividly illustrated perceptions regarding stability and support on the part of those leading the cooperation dialogue.[6]

Multiple interests within a country may thwart movement toward a deal.[7] Sometimes, especially in federal states, one region or province of a country may have a major stake in the sharing of the basin; their support may be critical in ratifying or implementing the agreement. This was the case in India with the signing of the Ganges agreement with Bangladesh—support from the state of West Bengal was critical to moving forward. A similar situation was present in the Columbia basin, where British Columbia voted against the agreement until some of its interests were recognized.

Sometimes multiple interests are evident at the national level. In many of the countries studied, Ministries of Water and the Ministries of Foreign Affairs had to align their views. The former focused on water infrastructure and hydrology, while the latter emphasized rights and equity. Similar differences also existed between Ministries of Water and Ministries of Energy, with the latter more concerned with power pools and interconnections than with water agreements.[8] Often, the variables that affect this category of risk may have nothing to do with water or with the offer on the table, but rather with the broader swath of issues that makes up local and regional politics.

Core versus Operational Risks

The five types of risks that we have identified can be grouped into two broader categories of risks: core or strategic risks, and operational risks. Sovereignty and Equity, deeply embedded in the economy and culture of the countries, are core risks that are more difficult to eliminate. Sovereignty and Equity risks may become more acute as more countries become involved in a cooperation deal, but these risks are apparent even in bilateral relationships. They tend to resurface even after agreements have been sealed and delivered, reflecting the visceral nature of these risks.

In three of the five cases, the return of concerns related to sovereignty and equity posed repeated implementation challenges for the agreement signed or for the agreed cooperative arrangement. It seems safe to assume that an agreement or a deal would allow breathing space to address the next round of sovereignty and equity concerns. The other three risk categories—capacity, accountability, and stability—pose similar challenges, but they seem to be more susceptible to operational interventions, which are discussed in chapters 4 and 5. These risk categories often feed into and influence the sovereignty and equity risks.

Notes

1. In the basin-wide Applied Training Project (ATP) in the Nile, some of the countries specifically asked for additional access to training benefits in order to "level the playing field."

2. The development of master plans and updates took a backseat in the 1990s in view of the preoccupation with competing priorities for management and development.

3. As per the Convention on the Law of the Non-navigational Uses of International Watercourses (United Nations 1997).

4. See *The Economist* (2011): "The Mekong River Commission, like ASEAN itself, is about consultation, process and consensus. No member is prepared to cede its national sovereignty, even on an issue as patently transnational as the Mekong."

5. See, for instance, Wouters (2000).

6. See the International Commission for the Protection of the Danube River (2006); personal communications with Al Duda and Ivan Zavadsky of the Global Environmental Facility.

7. See Waterbury (2002) for a detailed discussion of national interests.

8. The "power basins" often differed from "water basins" bringing a new set of stakeholders into play.

References

The Economist. 2011. "One Dam Thing after Another." November 13.

GFID (The German Foundation for International Development). 1998. "Transboundary Water Management: Experience of International River and Lake Commissions: Berlin Recommendations." http://www.umweltdaten.de /wasser-e/twmb98.pdf.

International Commission for the Protection of the Danube River. 2006. "15 Years of Managing the Danube River Basin." Vienna, Austria.

Rahaman, M. M. 2009. "Principles of Transboundary Water Resources Management and Ganges Treaties: An Analysis." *Water Resources Development* 25 (1): 159–73.

Salman, M. A., and K. Uprety. 2002. *Conflict and Cooperation on South Asia's International Rivers.* Washington, DC: World Bank.

United Nations. 1997. Convention on the Law of the Non-navigational Uses of International Watercourses. UN General Assembly Resolution 51/229.

Waterbury John. 2002. *The Nile Basin: National Determinants of Collective Action.* New Haven: Yale University Press.

Wouters, P. 2000. "The Relevance and Role of Water Law in the Sustainable Development of Freshwater: From Hydrosovereignty to Hydrosolidarity." *Water International* 25 (2): 200–7.

CHAPTER 4

Enhancing Cooperation

Countries that perceive risks to be too high may be moved to pursue appropriate risk reduction or opportunity-enhancing actions to a point where they decide to cooperate. Action by countries or third parties moves countries north on the y-axis of the analytical framework.

Reducing Risk

Risk reduction enters into cooperation decisions in that actions to reduce the level of perceived risk increase the attractiveness of cooperation offers. We identified specific interventions from the cases studied, which, like the risks themselves, we have broadly categorized. Overall, we list the following seven risk reduction strategies. Each risk reduction strategy addresses one or more of our five broad perceived risks. Table 4.1 provides an overview of the strategies.

A detailed discussion of how the seven broad strategies were manifested in the cases follows. This inventory is meant to be illustrative rather than exhaustive. Figure 4.1 illustrates the connections we found between a perceived risk and effective strategies for reducing that risk. The point is that when countries or partners are designing risk reduction strategies, linking them to the risks present will help ensure that the strategy is

Table 4.1   Seven Categories of Risk Reduction

Knowledge and skill expansion
Providing training and studies to meet gaps in capacity and knowledge and support for
  developing new skills
Institutional design
Tailoring the institutional arrangement to be a "fit-for-purpose" cooperative arrangement for
  dialogue and action among riparians
Agreement design
Tailoring the agreement to the preferences of political leaders involved in terms of its
  formality, scope, goals, and obligations.
Program design
Shaping the program to address country interests and goals, including sectoral links, long-
  term versus short-term benefits, and review and monitoring
Financing and guarantee
Meeting financing needs and gaps identified by countries, including third party guarantee of
  financial obligations
Facilitation (third party)
Providing unbiased, third party assistance in dialogues among riparians, including clarifica-
  tions and interpretations
Decision legitimacy
Using of consultation and discussion forums and other avenues for ensuring widespread
  domestic and regional support of decisions

Figure 4.1   Matching Risk Reduction Strategies to Risks

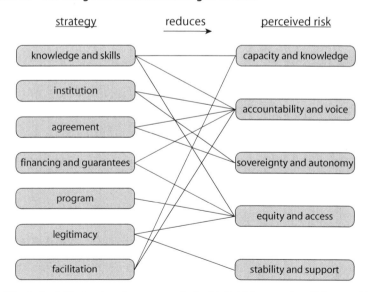

Note: Risk reduction (left) categories as they correspond to the risks (right) they can reduce. While some of the
major links between the two are highlighted, many additional links may be identified.

devised appropriately. A specific strategy may address more than one risk. A set of strategies may be needed to effectively deal with a specific risk. It is also clear from the analysis that often a mix of risk reduction strategies will be needed for every country, sometimes even the entire range discussed. In complex situations, a substantial portfolio of risk reduction strategies is requisite.

Knowledge and Skill Expansion
The objective is to meet gaps in capacity and knowledge within the countries. Key elements include specific tailor-made training and study tours; technical studies and fact versus fiction exercises; just-in-time notes for the technical and political leadership; and targeted briefs.

It is usually the case that a river basin is not well understood by the countries themselves and by third parties. Even where detailed studies are available, these may be outdated or new models and tools (for example, Geographic Information Systems (GIS)-based methodologies) may be used to obtain a much richer and more accurate picture of the hydrologic, economic, social, and environmental dimensions of the basin. Such new studies may persuade the countries to discard some of their perceived risks, both in terms of the size of the problem and the exposure to it. Don Blackmore (2011) advocates the use of studies that challenge prevalent myths with evidence-based analysis as countries engage in regional dialogue. Distinguishing between facts and misconceptions is critical to boost countries' knowledge of their river basins. Third parties have an opportunity to engage with decision makers to identify myths and communicate facts. Because long-held beliefs are not easily dispelled, time and active involvement of the countries in the process will be key.

Just-in-time notes or timely briefs can inform ministerial decision making. In one of the cases, a review of global experiences in river basin institutions helped to advance the understanding of the ministers as they evaluated their next steps. Much care must be taken to ensure just-in-time notes are not perceived as leading to a process dominated by third parties; the notes are a useful guidance tool, but ministers rather than third parties make the actual decisions. Specific questions may need targeted research and output to aid decision making. Examples of these in the cases included the selection of the chief executive; the sequencing of investments; and the operating rules for water infrastructure. Study tours also served as useful forums for free exchanges outside one's own river basin when they were well-structured and organized as study seminars.

Support for developing new skills in advancing the knowledge agenda (for example, in modeling or hydrology) or for needed action (for example, stakeholder consultation, project planning, or project finance) could be equally critical.[1] Given skepticism of analyses conducted by "outsiders" to the basin, it is important to identify, motivate, and strengthen the institutions and individuals within the respective river basin in the use of modern tools and techniques.

Institutional Design

The objective is to design a cooperative arrangement for dialogue and action among riparian countries in line with the preferences of the political leadership. It is best not to rely on blueprints but rather to search for solutions for situations. Achievement of this objective will depend on several elements of institutional design, including the following:

- *Mandate and scope of work of the cooperative mechanism.* This element pertains to questions such as whether there is a role for the regional cooperative mechanism with respect to water resources management, water development, other sectors, basin planning, investment preparation and implementation, coordination, financial management, monitoring, information sharing, and dispute settlement. Decisions about the mandate and scope of work seem to depend on the comfort level of the political leadership to entrust certain functions to the cooperative arrangement.

- *Degree of the formality or informality of the organizational arrangement.* The political leadership in the cases studied did not follow a model or blueprint for all occasions. For instance, the Niger basin governments assigned a coordinating and cooperative planning role to the Niger Basin Authority, unlike the stronger powers of the neighboring Senegal River Basin Authority. The Nile Basin Initiative (NBI) was a transitional mechanism and did not have powers for joint management of the river.

- *Governance and decision-making setup of the cooperative mechanism.* The Ganges Treaty included an elaborate structure of layered decision-making levels during its implementation. The NBI included technical and political layers of decision making for its governance, together with several consultative mechanisms for advisory inputs. The Niger Basin Authority's governance included these, in addition to periodic meetings of heads of states for strategic decisions.

- *Crucial rules of engagement for trust building and perception of balance among the countries.* The decision-making process was often consultative, and a one-country, one-vote system was followed irrespective of the size of the country or share of the basin. Rules conveyed confirmation of cooperation in action and contributed to confidence building.[2]

Agreement Design

The objective is to design a "fit for purpose" agreement related to the purposes of inter-country cooperation, given the preferences of the political leadership. Key elements include the principles espoused by the agreement; its degree of formality or informality; its scope and content, including its references to overall goals of the agreement; rights and obligations of countries; its predictability; procedures for information sharing, dispute resolution, and effecting changes; duration of the agreement; and modes of bringing the agreement into operational status. Institutional design is also often a feature of agreements though differentiated for the sake of analysis.

Agreements and institutions in the cases demonstrated a range of characteristics. They could be legally binding or nonbinding. They could be very formal or nonformal (that is, along a spectrum from a signed treaty to a verbal understanding or handshake). They could start as a nonformal cooperative arrangement and develop into a more formal type as confidence is built and when the political leadership is ready. The Syr Darya Agreement was a framework agreement with the hope of further subsidiary agreements. The Niger Basin Agreement, which included measures for notification and review, was later supplemented by a strong Water Charter that specified how interventions by one country on the Niger River could be pursued. The Ganges Treaty followed years of temporary memoranda of understanding in the 1970s and 1980s. The NBI was based on the signed minutes of the Ministers of Water Affairs and subsequent decisions by these ministers on its governance and decision-making process. Two of the agreements dealt with sharing of water quantity.

In other words, cooperative arrangements have to fit the context and riparian preferences. Bilder (1981) catalogues an impressive inventory of nonformal to formal agreements and measures to make them work in the context of international agreements. Similarly, Fischhendler (2008a) describes how ambiguity in agreements can be useful, as well as counterproductive (2008b). As in the case of institutional design, agreements may become more formalized as trust and confidence grow or events and circumstances motivate the countries to make changes in existing arrangements. The evolution of the Niger basin's regional entity from a commission in the 1960s to an authority in later years is an apt illustration of such evolution.

Program Design

The objective is to present a program responding to the interests of the countries in line with their goals for development and cooperation. Key interventions toward this objective include the following:

- *Shaping the program's objectives, components, detailing of benefits and costs, mode of design, and delivery to address country interests.* This was exemplified by the Niger Basin Authority, which launched a long-term program of development (the Sustainable Development Action Program [SDAP] and a related Investment Program [IP]). This program specified the types of benefit flows that could be expected over a 20-year period, making clear the size, sequence, and timing ("who-gets-what-when-and-how much") question at the heart of many dissensions in international waters programs. The protracted negotiations among the Eastern Nile riparians also ended with an identified set of projects accommodating the interests of the three countries. Clarity in the program not only demonstrated benefit flows to a county but also to other countries. It was thus possible to get a sense of relative benefits. Some attribute the lack of such a program in the past as a disincentive in Zambezi cooperation.

- *Clarifying ways of making changes in the program and monitoring and reporting.* At the time, the Ganges Treaty was considered an improvement over what was prevalent in terms of monitoring and dispute settlement.[3] In the other basins, annual reviews offered the chance to share a transparent picture of benefit and cost flows.

- *Linking benefits within a sector, or between or among sectors, or with the national economy or politics.* The Syr Darya Agreement extended to water and power and responded to fiscal conditions, all critical in the post-Soviet period for the Central Asian economies. The Eastern Nile Program extended to energy, flood, and watershed management. The Ganges Treaty carried the promise of future agreements on other shared rivers between India and Bangladesh. Thus, dialogue on cooperation on water could be linked to benefits within the water sector or to other sectors in the national economy.[4]

Financing, including Guarantees

The objective is to meet the financing needs and gaps identified in the institutional and program design and agreed to by the countries. Demonstration of funds flows provides a reassurance that the promised benefits that need capital would, in fact, become a reality. This need was very pronounced in the Eastern Nile and Niger, where countries emphasized the need to move from plans to action.

In Niger, countries were moving into plans for concrete action after over 30 years and were impatient to see positive results from cooperation. Financing was not a key element of the Ganges Treaty, proof that risk reduction measures should not follow a blueprint and should target specific risks in a basin at a given time.

Key elements in financing include the following:

- Addressing the challenge of financing the agreed program through a detailed component-wise analysis of resource needs and gaps.

- Identifying and locating sources of financing, mobilizing financing partners, and obtaining commitments. These sources could include the riparian countries themselves, other countries, external bilateral and multilateral partners, private sector sponsors, and financiers. The SDAP and the IP of the Niger basin narrowed their focus to the first phase covering eight years and costing $1.8 billion, and the NBA set about mobilizing support for that phase. The Eastern Nile investment program was presented to donors in 2001 and commitments of support were obtained.

- Providing support for regional public goods, that is, cooperative institutions. In view of the observations that the presence of cooperative mechanisms and their robustness served the ends of conflict prevention and resolution, it is in the interest of the countries and their friends to create and sustain such public goods. However, the costs of establishing and sustaining them can be significant. In the cases reviewed, a combination of country and bilateral and international donor partners financed them over substantial periods of time, often for a decade or more.

- Financing the process itself. These long-term processes can be extremely costly and this must be a consideration during the drafting of finance and investment plans. In particular, there must be support for the many costs of development teams, the leasing of venues for negotiations, and the time of ministerial staff and advisers.

The size of financing required in each of the cases points to the need for multiple sources and hence to the need for a coordinated approach among financiers. None of the cases indicated evidence of guarantee arrangements, although some may be used in the future.

Third-Party Facilitation

The objective is to assist the riparian dialogue as an unbiased third party. Key elements include the following: facilitating inter-country exchanges; interpreting each other's interests; helping to clarify mutually beneficial cooperation opportunities; extending assurances regarding the flow of cooperation benefits; and ensuring effective implementation of institutional mechanisms, agreements, and the program. Donor partners were associated with four of the five cases at the request of the countries.

In the case of the Niger basin, the partners signed a declaration of support in 2004 in parallel for the countries resolving to pursue cooperative management of the river. Where necessary and invited, partners have facilitated dialogue among countries. In the case of the Eastern Nile, partners have responded to specific requests for facilitative assistance, especially in the formative years. The United States Agency for International Development (USAID) took the lead in Syr Darya; the Nordic countries took the lead in the Zambezi. It is important for the countries to see third parties as truly neutral and possessing the capacity to convene stakeholders and mobilize resources.

Decision Legitimacy

The objective is to ensure widespread support for decisions on cooperation. Key interventions include providing forums for discussion with official and civil society at national and regional levels; modifying strategies taking stakeholder inputs into account; ensuring legitimacy at the highest levels of political leadership (ministerial, heads of state); and allowing for inter-sectoral and inter-ministerial consensus.

Approvals for next steps in the Nile and Niger were obtained at the ministerial level and at the chief executive level. In the Niger, heads of state met periodically to address strategic issues and approve decisions. In Bangladesh and India, the highest levels of political leadership at federal and state government levels were involved in the Ganges Treaty.[5]

Participants in the case situations referred to the need for a healthy national and international discourse to present country interests, discuss alternatives, and identify winners and losers in cooperative deals. The Nile 2002 conferences did provide a regional platform for the forceful exchange of country viewpoints by academics and civil society organizations. Such exchanges to generate options to the status quo within the countries would be needed to strengthen the legitimacy of the final decision. Fostering national debates, with the participation of civil society organizations, on sensitive and strategic issues around water may not be possible in some countries. However, strategic communication by leaders to their domestic constituents throughout the process can help them to gain and retain internal support.

Table 4.2 outlines an indicative set of key risk reduction strategies employed in each of the case studies.

Building Opportunity

Our analysis suggests that political opportunity is a critical factor in decisions to cooperate or not over shared water resources. In all of our cases, there was some evidence of the role of opportunity in moving countries to cooperate; in some, opportunity seemed to be the driving force. Countries may see a political opportunity, seize it, and move to risk reduction to finalize a cooperation agreement. Or, in the process of understanding the risks and exploring risk reduction measures, countries may see new political opportunities in engaging in cooperative deals.

At times, we found that political opportunity trumped residual risk. For example, leaders in both Bangladesh and India moved forward with the Ganges Water Sharing Treaty despite some domestic resistance. The Arab Republic of Egypt and Ethiopia entered into an agreement despite remaining risks. The Kyrgyz Republic and Uzbekistan signed the Syr Darya agreement with almost no risks removed. In all of these cases, the decision makers saw new opportunities due to regional changes in geopolitics or global paradigm shifts.

Table 4.2 Illustrative Risk Reduction Strategies by Basin

Risk Reduction	Eastern Nile	Ganges	Niger	Syr Darya	Zambezi
Knowledge and skills	Studies including modeling part of the basin Capacity building through basin-wide program, as well as at country level Just-in-time notes	Detailed studies of water flows; lack of updated information led to concerns later about use of old data	Specific capacity building program through bilateral and collective effort of partners Briefs and notes on institutional develop-ment, communication, modeling, river basin organizations	Studies (modeling), study tours, and technical assistance	Training offered in planning and negotiations at country and regional levels Studies on basin development options Strengthening of national level transboundary management functions
Institutional design	Interim organization in line with mandate of the Nile Basin Initiative (NBI). Some permanence through HQ Agreement for the Eastern Nile Technical Regional Office (ENTRO) Designation as a "Technical Office" met all interests Role of ENTRO in national and regional agendas addressed	Layered decision making, including technical and political leadership	Revitalization needed and done; reform study done and approved by heads of state Balance assured	Reliance on an available mechanism —the Syr Darya Basin Organization	Interim arrangement while treaty being crafted
Third-party facilitation	Partners committed to funding immediate program in June 2001 in response to request by the three countries	Bilateral	Partners support through facilitation, technical assistance, studies, and financing	Partners help with technical assistance through studies (modeling and capacity building	Partners active

72

Financing	Financing sought for all activities			Partners funding of TA and training
Design of the agreement	Interim agreement Mandate to only advance minister-approved program Broad general objectives—an "agreement to agree" on working together	Long term to convey predictability Formal agreement Framework for future agreements for other rivers in the basin	Partners helped with first phase of IP Framework with protocols that would follow later	Framework agreement Water, energy, and economy linked	Interim arrangement while the treaty was being crafted; interim secretariat
Program design	Responsive to interests of countries Short-term results, long-term promises, backed by studies Specific activities to satisfy each country	Specification of water-sharing formula	The SDAP and IP include specific projects and timing and sequence of various activities, specifying who gets what and when		Mostly studies and training, some ongoing coordination activities
Decision legitimacy	Ministries of foreign affairs and heads of state involved Inter-country exchange through various forums; less debate within the country	Federal, state, and civil society discussions; some dissent between federal and state governments and within civil society Highest levels of political leadership engaged	Nongovernmental organizations involved		Many opportunities for consultations and discussions at national and regional levels

Political opportunity is therefore an important consideration in cooperation in international waters. Through such opportunities, countries and political leaders may pursue the following:

- *Seek or declare their alliance or solidarity with a country or a group of countries.* Soon after independence, the Niger basin countries formed the Niger Basin Commission, partly as a declaration of regional solidarity and independence.
- *Raise their regional and global profile.* The objective is to change or strengthen the current image of the country in regional or global politics. India's motivation in the Ganges Treaty was triggered by its new foreign policy and was aimed at enhancing regional relations.

In such situations, a political opportunity can be seen as a "door opener" for cooperation decisions. Nevertheless, risk reduction measures may still be needed to convert the opportunity into a cooperative deal. In all of the cases where political opportunity motivated regional cooperation, specific risk reduction measures were still essential for the shaping and adoption of practical—and sustainable—agreements.

Various Paths to Cooperation

The diversity of risk reduction strategies needed in fostering cooperative deals is further exemplified by examining the diversity of "paths to cooperation" taken by countries. For example, our analysis found some situations where risk reduction is a primary step, and others where benefit or opportunity expansion preceded risk reduction. Figure 4.2 illustrates the various paths toward cooperation, using the Risks and Opportunities to Cooperation Framework.

There are two major implications of the "different paths":

- The variety of risk reduction strategies usually needed, in line with the variety of paths to cooperation, provides a strong rationale for partners to coordinate or pool their assistance efforts in international waters rather than extend support separately. The work on cooperation in international waters is too vast for single-handed support.
- Solutions will have to be customized for a specific situation, following careful assessments. Blueprint solutions from "model" river basins are unlikely to work.

Figure 4.2   Paths to Cooperation

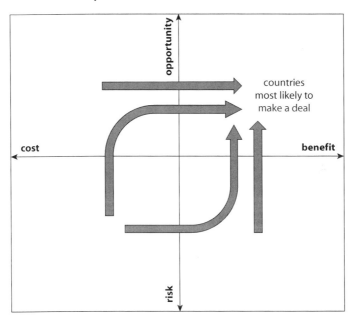

Notes: When countries consider costs, benefits, risks, and opportunities, they are positioned in one of the four quadrants on the Risks and Opportunities to Cooperation framework. To move to the northeast quadrant, a combination of risk reduction, opportunity enhancement, and benefit expansion sends them along various trajectories.

Notes

1. Countries, as well as the World Bank and development partners, have many existing decision support tools, including regional hydrologic models.
2. See the discussion on the accountability risk earlier in this chapter.
3. Complaints have arisen since then.
4. See Dombrowsky (2010) for an interesting perspective on intra- and inter-sectoral links in deal making in water; and Sadoff and Grey (2002) on the benefits beyond water.
5. Some countries require parliamentary approvals for international treaties.

References

Bilder, R. B. 1981. *Managing the Risks of International Agreement.* Madison, WI: University of Wisconsin Press.

Blackmore, D. 2011. "The Water Story: Application to Other Areas." Presentation at the Australian Water Day, World Bank, Washington, DC, January 31.

Dombrowsky, I. 2010. "The Role of Intra-Water Sector Issue Linkage in the Resolution of Transboundary Water Conflicts." *Water International* 35 (2): 132–49.

Fischhendler, I. 2008a. "Ambiguity in Transboundary Environmental Dispute Resolution: The Israeli-Jordanian Water Agreement." *Journal of Peace Research* 45: 91.

———. 2008b. "When Ambiguity in Treaty Design Becomes Destructive: A Study of Transboundary Water." *Global Environmental Politics* 8 (1): 115.

Sadoff, C., and D. Grey. 2002. "Beyond the River: The Benefits of Cooperation on International Rivers." *Water Policy* 4 (5): 389–403.

CHAPTER 5

Pointers for Partners

Partners are attracted to river basin cooperation by the principles of integrated water resources management and the goal of conflict prevention. The partners consider regional cooperation to be a valuable public good[1] and feel they could play an external facilitator and honest broker role. Accordingly, they act individually or collectively to support riparian countries in advancing the cooperation agenda. In this chapter, we discuss pointers for partner action for facing risks and identifying opportunities. The intention of this chapter is to provide insight and ideas for use in conjunction with tools already available and in use. Providing the most stable platform possible for countries to work through their own issues is paramount throughout the process of third-party involvement. Partners should consider these pointers while continuing to emphasize the commitment to long-term goals, reasonable expectations, steadiness, and flexibility.

Specific Partner Actions

Figure 5.1 shows a suggested chronology of partner actions discussed in this section. Since the goal is for countries to do much of this work on their own, the figure illustrates where and how partners can play a role

Figure 5.1 Timeline of Suggested Partner Actions

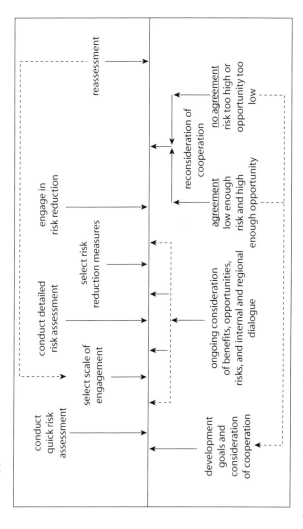

Notes: The succession of potential partner interventions in risk assessment and risk reduction are shown on the top half of the figure, with ongoing country considerations and actions are shown on the bottom half. This placement does not imply that countries are unable to take these actions themselves. Rather, it is a guide for partners wishing to engage with willing countries. Periodic reassessments are needed, making this an iterative process. The figure also shows how much time and effort are needed in moving to a deal.

at the request of the countries. In addition, the various steps of partner action are discussed.

Quick Assessment

The starting point is a baseline assessment of the benefits and risks of cooperation in international waters. Discussions of projected benefits with countries will alert partners to the risks seen by the countries in accessing those benefits through any deals for cooperative action. We suggest that this assessment be done in two phases: a preliminary analysis and a detailed assessment. During the first phase, a Quick Assessment would involve a stock-taking of the perception of all of the countries based on the available literature and experience. Such an assessment could highlight the benefits, risks, and opportunities, and thereby offer guidance as to the preferred scale of engagement of development partners. The Quick Assessment is not a substitute for a thorough assessment, but instead a starting point.

Choosing the Scale of Engagement

Global dialogue has promoted cooperation in international waters to the extent that it is often difficult to discount the full basin as the appropriate unit with which to engage. Nevertheless, partners should question whether basin level engagement would be a fruitful exercise in specific situations, despite its desirability from the viewpoint of the principles of integrated water resources management. For instance:

- A country may pursue its development goals, but it could have access to its own sources or private sources of financing for its development program. The country may not see cooperation as a means of accessing capital, and indeed it may only see substantial risks in cooperative activities. Its preferred route may be unilateral action for water development or management.

- Partners may conclude their Quick Assessment and find that the degree of conflict among the countries is too intense due to geopolitical factors or that the level of mistrust among countries is extremely high. There could be a reproduction of various bilateral and sub-regional conflicts at the basin level. Thus, the political context may not offer a positive climate for engagement at the basin level.

- Issues around cooperation may be so strategic that there is no room for third-party action. Countries may consider information and issues around international waters as highly classified or falling entirely within the domain of sovereign governments, with no space for outside parties such as partners (Earle, Jägerskog, and Öjendal 2010).

In these situations, engaging on a sub-basin or country level to build cooperation from below may be more appropriate. For instance, several bilateral agreements preceded the revitalization of the Niger Basin Authority (NBA), indicating that much confidence building had occurred before the NBA was reformed. Efforts to demonstrate the benefits of cooperation and to analyze perceived risks may still be worthwhile actions for partners at a country or sub-basin level. In particular, building the knowledge base through analytical studies and stimulating country exposure to successful experiences of cooperation would be good background and preparation in case an opportunity for cooperation arises.

Selecting the appropriate scale of engagement is an important decision, since each level demands different time horizons of commitment, levels of complexity, amounts of resources, and types of expertise. There is not necessarily one "correct" scale to target in each situation—in fact, some basins may benefit most from multi-scale engagement. The intensity of engagement at each level—country, cluster of countries, sub-basin, or basin—could vary depending on the situation in the basin. Even when there is intense activity at the sub-basin level, other less intense activities, for example, capacity building or climate risk studies, could be pursued. The point is to determine which levels of engagement are optimal for the given situation, for example, where the levels of the receptiveness of the countries and the effectiveness of support are both relatively high.

When, and whether, to move between scales is also an important decision. Since much of this decision will depend on political opportunity, it is important for partners to remain in tune with regional geopolitics. Also, as cooperation is itself an iterative process, periodic reassessments will be crucial. Partner strategy may change as driven by the results of the assessments.

Detailed Assessment of Risks and Risk Reduction Measures

Once the scale of engagement is determined, a second phase of analysis would include detailed assessments of risks, followed by discussions with the concerned countries. A careful analysis is critical in order to choose the most useful risk reduction strategies. The level of difficulty associated with this process will vary. In some cases, a country may clearly articulate its perception and the risk may be fairly easy to identify. In other cases, a country may speak about a particular risk, but discussions with the country and careful "listening" may point to another concern that is preoccupying the country. Dialogue and due diligence will be needed to fully understand all of the risks the country faces. This report offers guidance on the types of risks commonly found.

Once the set of risks is clearly identified, the selection of a risk reduction strategy calls for reviewing the menu of options and selecting the applicable package of interventions. Partners may choose from the seven risk reduction strategies presented in chapter 4 in this book. Partners can find potential roles for themselves with respect to each type of risk reduction strategy. In the case of complex multi-country settings, third-party facilitation is a particularly critical function and partners are well-disposed to carry out or support such a function.

It will be important to seek validation from experts on the selected measures. The advice of a selected number of regional specialists and political leaders to review and validate—and revisit if necessary—the detailed assessment for accuracy is critical. Their knowledge of the basin situation and input on the risk analysis and risk reduction strategy will help a great deal. A way to access such expertise is through the formation of an advisory group of two to three members who are knowledgeable about the basin and the countries involved. This group can be called upon to validate the findings of the assessment and the type of risk reduction measures identified. Partner agencies may also have such regional specialists on their rolls.

Providing Risk Reduction Support to Countries

Third parties can actively engage countries in risk reduction. Table 5.1 provides examples from our cases for interventions related to each of the seven risk reduction strategies. We elaborate on three of the measures of knowledge and skill building, financing, and third-party facilitation and guarantee.

Knowledge and skill building. Partners can support the preparation of new studies or updates of old studies that identify basin-wide biophysical, economic, environmental, and social characteristics, as well as water availability, current use, and expected demand and supply. Modeling can examine a variety of scenarios of further availability, use and demand, and changing features of the basin, including the cumulative impacts of investments and land use strategies and the impacts of climate variability and change. Frontier study areas need funding and intellectual support. During the

Table 5.1   Illustrative Risk Reduction Support Measures

Strategy	Specific Intervention	Major Lesson
Institutional Design	Nile Basin Initiative (NBI) was a transitional arrangement, and was not mandated to manage Nile waters. The revitalization of the Nile Basin Authority (NBA) included a major institutional reform program and the infusion of the NBA's formal structure with people and processes that made it work. Interim secretariat set up for Zambezi Watercourses Commission Agreement (ZAMCOM) in the absence of a formal agreement among Zambezi countries.	The regional institution must respond to the desired intensity of cooperation and needs of the political leadership at a given time.
Agreement Design	NBI was a "light agreement" with few obligations and with ease of exit. The 30-year duration of the bilateral deal between India and Bangladesh provided some predictability. The NBA Agreement provided for notification and review. The Syr Darya agreement linked salient regional issues of water and energy.	The strength, duration, and content of an agreement must respond to countries' needs and the regional geopolitical climate.
Program Design	A package of investments organized for the Eastern Nile accommodated the interests of all the countries. NBA program clearly reflected the size, sequence, and flow of benefits to the countries. ZAMCOM's program did not include a clear portfolio of investments. The Syr Darya program accommodated the needs of the upstream and downstream countries.	It is useful to demonstrate the types of benefits that will accrue and a transparent means for the countries to understand relative gains.
Financing and Guarantees	Multilateral and bilateral funds for the NBI were mobilized through a consultative group and later through a multi-donor trust fund as well as regular investment channels.	Demonstrating financial support reassures benefits will accrue. A financing plan makes transparent the details of funds flow.

	Commitments were obtained for the first phase of the Eastern Nile Subsidiary Action Program Investment Program. Financing of development needs not spelled out in the Zambezi program.	
Third-party Facilitation	The World Bank and partners were present at the NBI table and offered facilitation services as requested. The World Bank and partners signed a parallel charter of support to the country led Niger Basin Program. Minimal direct third-party involvement in the Ganges. The United States Agency for International Development provided facilitation, capacity building, and some financing in the Syr Darya.	Partners can offer helpful third-party support, if countries request it. Honest third-party brokering can play a critical role.
Decision Legitimacy	Approval for advancing the Eastern Nile program was obtained at the ministerial level as well as at the highest political level, for example, prime minister. Heads of state approved NBA's revitalization strategy and the Sustainable Development Action Plan and Investment Plan (SDAP/IP). Highest levels of political leadership were involved in India and Bangladesh—both federal and provincial level endorsements allowed for a more stable agreement.	Broad-based support for cooperative deals helps with agreement stability. National discourse and civil society participation are important in the long term.
Expanding Knowledge and Skill	Parallel Nile basin-wide programs were launched for capacity building and strengthening functions at the country level. Studies and modeling carried out in preparation for NBA's SDAP demonstrated basin development scenarios and potential impacts on the river. Several studies identified strategies for integrated water resources management in the Zambezi but failed to level country capacities.	Appropriate studies and fact building can help countries see the benefits and discount them to set aside some risks.

period of dialogue among countries, there will be many occasions that will benefit from just-in-time notes and analysis. Confidential critiques may be required. The Global Environment Facility (GEF) supported Transboundary Diagnostic Analysis and Strategic Action Plan, which have proven useful avenues for advancing studies and dialogue in international waters. These instruments have been effectively used in the Aral Sea, Mekong, Niger, and Senegal basins. Donor support for advancing knowledge has been particularly useful in long neglected technical and engineering feasibility studies and in exploring new specialty areas such as benefits sharing analysis, environmental flows, impacts of climate variability and change, strategic environmental and social analysis, and cumulative impacts analysis.

Similarly, partners have a long tradition of supporting a variety of capacity building activities in international rives. With reference to cooperation, the development of transboundary capacities within the water ministries and incorporation of considerations of international waters in national policies are areas in which partners could provide support. Specific skill building in selected fields such as negotiation, modeling, communication, and regional impact analysis has been a welcome area for partners' support to riparian countries.

Third-party facilitation. In cases in which riparian countries seek third-party facilitation, partners could play significant roles. Cooperative management in river basins usually take time, often decades. Countries generally move in nonlinear paths from unilateral to cooperative action. At various stages, third-party facilitation can help in aiding interaction and communication across borders and across national, thematic, and sectoral boundaries within and across countries. A neutral country, a development partner, or a private sector sponsor could facilitate dialogue. This facilitation will require the ability of the country, partner, or sponsor to organize, convene, and mediate various types of interaction at various levels and at various times, complemented by studies and technical assistance. Listening skills on the part of third-party facilitators will be critical.

The line between facilitation and active diplomacy is not a sharp one. There may be tendencies (and temptations) to cross from one mode of engagement to the other. It is recommended that the team periodically reflect on its work and generate continuous feedback on style and substance of interaction between the partner and the countries.

Financing and guarantees. Identifying, mobilizing, and delivering financing for the cooperative program and related investments is an important risk reduction measure. Partners can act as conveners and financiers in support of riparian programs. In all the cases studies for this report, except in the Ganges, partners extended financial assistance ranging from grants to loans. Elsewhere, guarantees have been an effective means of completing the financial support package. Financing must be treated as an integral part of the support to riparians to complement other risk reduction measures, such as the preparation of the agreement and program design and to signal assurances that the expected benefits from cooperation will flow as planned.

A great deal of support for the countries will be needed in the early stages of cooperation. Such support is crucial for the start up of such complex ventures. In the past, several United Nations (UN) agencies, in particular the United Nations Development Programme (UNDP), have played stellar roles in supporting countries through the nascent stages of cooperation, especially after Rio 1992. Some of the bilateral and multilateral donor agencies have also invested heavily in invaluable start-up efforts. GEF's instruments in international waters are a helpful means of getting started.[2]

Additional Considerations

Coordinating Support
Given the multiplicity of interventions that may be needed to foster cooperation, especially in high-risk situations, a coordinated approach to partner support has much merit. It is also desirable in view of the generally long time needed (10 to 20 years) for cooperation endeavors to bear fruit and the need to build on the comparative strengths and capacities of the partners.

A helpful way forward for partners would be to coordinate their support to the countries. Without being idealistic about "harmonization,"[3] coordination of support would assist countries with a range of interventions that may be needed, especially in the case of high-risk situations. An example is the Nile Basin Trust Fund, a multi-donor resource pool aligned to the objectives and programs of the Nile countries, established by partners in 2003 and executed by the World Bank.[4] The Cooperation Framework signed by partners in April 2004, following the declaration of commitment by the Niger basin countries to sustainable and cooperative development of the shared river, is a slightly different, but equally workable, example. Partners agreed on a set of principles, then directed their financial and technical assistance directly to the Niger Basin Authority

(NBA) rather than through a common pool, periodically engaging in dialogue with one another to maximize coordination of their efforts. Both the Nile and Niger programs motivate partners to align their efforts with riparian priorities.

The coordinated approach also offers the chance to capitalize on mutual strengths. Some partners are better able to act as conveners, others as project financiers, and others as knowledge facilitators. All of these strengths and capacities are needed during the long road to cooperation in international waters. It is cost-effective to coordinate and tap comparative strengths in aiding countries moving in the direction of cooperation.

Dealing with Intra-Agency Issues

Cooperation deals are desirable, yet the outcomes of efforts to foster cooperation are full of uncertainties. High-level champions within partner agencies will have to take ownership of such efforts, legitimize partner support within the agencies, and commit the agencies to such activities, even while facing the probability of failures and setbacks in cooperation in international waters. Such a scenario also implies the need for selectivity since it is close to impossible to deal with several river basins and countries at the same time.

The time needed and the uncertainties of results could be highly demotivating for work teams. Quick results are not realistic expectations, given the perceived risks discussed earlier.[5] Accordingly, process outcomes such as rules of engagement, institutional development, and preparation of plans may have to be legitimized alongside more concrete development outcomes, especially in the early years of cooperation. Monitoring and evaluation should receive significant attention at the planning stage. Results frameworks may often need to give special attention to "what success looks like" in the work on international waters during an evolving process of cooperation. Communication of outputs and outcomes is critical for teams engaged in international waters, particularly in view of the length of time needed and the uncertainties of outcomes.

Anticipating Opportunity

Political opportunity is an important consideration in cooperation in international waters. The dilemma is that political opportunity is unpredictable and often depends on issues outside of the water arena. For example, a change in regime can shift a country's position on a particular agreement. Shift in trade patterns can influence cooperation in water.

Identifying and seizing political opportunities are activities that are largely in the domain of political leaders in the riparian countries.

Are there actions that partners can take to advance opportunities? This is not clear to us from the cases. Surely, staying on top of geopolitics of the basin is important for those promoting cooperation. Partners can track and monitor political developments and analyze the expected effects of global and regional geopolitics on national policy making. They can stand ready to extend support should leaders move to strike a deal. In addition, the types of questions partners might ask to enhance movement northward along the opportunity-enhancement axis would include the following:

- What makes a potential agreement politically palatable, or even desirable?
- How can institutional design or any other risk reduction strategy enhance the political favorability, and vice versa?

The nature of such opportunities in the context of international waters, and the options to enhance such opportunities, are areas for further investigation.

Dealing with the Dynamic Nature of Cooperation Deals

Our analysis indicates that cooperation is an iterative process in which the benefits and costs and the opportunities and risks are constantly changing and demanding of attention. At times, when cooperation occurs, whether because of substantial risk reduction measures, or because of a combination of risk reduction and political opportunity, it is not necessarily sustained far into the future. At other times, cooperative arrangements grow and evolve into robust institutions that not only stand the test of time but also evolve with the times. Thus, reassessments are essential over the long term—as situations change, identifying what is different will be an important step in sustaining or strengthening cooperation.

Often, progress is followed or accompanied by regression. Countries may take one step forward and two steps backward. Importantly, these backward steps can occur even after an agreement is reached, highlighting the fragile nature of international agreements. Furthermore, the flux in geopolitics and uncertainties of hydrology add a further dimension of complexity to cooperation and is a caution against seeking "permanent fixes" in cooperation deals. Accounting for the fragility and for the many uncertainties demands adaptability and flexibility in the cooperative arrangements. This accounting seems to be particularly important for the cases of cooperative agreements that involved detailed quantitative water sharing formulae.

However, even brief periods of cooperation can offer opportunities to implement projects or institutions that scale up cooperation to have lasting and long-term impacts. When hydropolitical relations are strained in a basin, evaluating potential interventions against political realities becomes imperative. Regardless of the current relations, activities designed to be both sensitive to existing realities and help move countries toward greater cooperation could be fruitful. Such cooperation-inducing interventions will need further careful reflection.

Systematic, Iterative Action

The Implementation Progress Report of the World Bank's Water Resources Sector Strategy (2003) noted the constraints and challenges of cooperation in international waters and observed: "Understanding the political economy dimensions of transboundary engagement through upstream analytical work, and technical assistance are critical in reducing the risk profile of investment projects. The challenge for those engaging in international waters work is to translate this advice into action."

The cases demonstrated a laudable sensitivity to the political economy dimension among partner teams working in international waters. Evidence of application of risk reduction measures to knotty situations in the cases attests to this observation. What appears to be needed is *a more systematic approach* to analyzing the risks and formulating a risk reduction strategy, including tapping expert advice. The approach should help teams identify appropriate rather than ideal, and flexible rather than permanent cooperative arrangements. We also need a clear understanding that the *risk analysis and support for risk reduction are iterative processes* and thus *continued and consistent action over time.*

Notes

1. See MFA (2001). This consultant report calls for an International Shared Waters Facility and for a broad range of support, while advocating support for sustained institutional development.

2. These have been used with very positive effects in the Niger and Senegal basins.

3. A political leader observed that he was excited that partners were willing to support the countries in international waters and added that, in turn, countries may have to help partners cooperate among themselves.

4. Of the 17 partners participating in the trust fund activities, 10 contribute to the fund and 7 do not. The latter directly finance the Nile Basin Initiative. Nevertheless, they participate in trust fund meetings to ensure a reasonable level of coordinated action.

5. Work on international waters is not recommended for those starting out on their water careers.

References

Earle, A., A. Jägerskog, and J. Öjendal, eds. 2010. *Transboundary Water Management: Principles and Practice.* London: Earthscan.

MFA (Sweden Ministry of Foreign Affairs). 2001. "Transboundary Water Management as an International Public Good." Study 2001:1, MFA, Stockholm.

World Bank. 2003. "The Water Resources Sector Strategy: Managing and Developing Water Resources to Reduce Poverty." World Bank, Washington, DC.

CHAPTER 6

Conclusion: Lessons Learned

The World Bank's Operational Policy on International Waterways calls for proactive action to foster cooperation in international waters: "The Bank recognizes that the cooperation and goodwill of riparians is essential for the efficient use and protection of the waterway. Therefore, it attaches great importance to riparians making appropriate agreements or arrangements for these purposes for the entire waterway or any part thereof. The Bank stands ready to assist riparians in achieving this end (World Bank 2001)."

The World Bank and partners have indeed shown a keen interest in supporting "riparians making appropriate· agreements or arrangements." This study reviewed a slice of the experience, by exploring related risks and mechanisms for reducing those risks to ultimately further cooperation based on a sample of cases. Chapter 2 exemplified the diversity of risks associated with engaging in cooperation over international waters. Chapters 3 and 4 presented a possible inventory of types of risks of cooperation perceived by countries and of related risk reduction strategies, and chapter 5 outlined potential steps for partners in promoting cooperation and reducing risks. This chapter presents key messages from the study. Figure 6.1 summarizes these messages.

Figure 6.1   Lessons Learned

On Risk and Risk Reduction

Risks are less studied but are critical in decision making. Several previous studies have focused on the economic benefits and costs to cooperation over water. Although more recent work has explored expanded benefits that can result from cooperation, little attention has been paid to the role of political economy in decision making and country perception of risks, in particular. Thus, this study addresses an important gap in knowledge on the topic of international waters.

Countries are not unitary actors; several stakeholders are likely to be involved. Sometimes, use of the term *country decision-making* can imply that a country is a unitary actor, thereby losing the diversity of interests within a country. It is important to recognize that dynamics within each country influence the likelihood of cooperation. Stakeholder voices and the national discourse are critical elements in the decision-making process.

Individual decision makers matter; champions are key. At times, it is the vision, will, charisma, or personal politics of a certain decision maker in a country that determines whether or not a deal is made. Motives of individual decision makers matter. By extension, the same is true of partners and teams as they set out to facilitate and support the cooperation process.

Solutions must be devised for situations; these solutions should match country needs. There is no blueprint or one-size-fits-all approach that will ensure success. Countries take different paths to cooperation. For partners, it is imperative to invest the necessary time and resources to produce the most appropriate solution possible for the situation at hand. Fit-for-purpose remedies rather than model river basin solutions are needed.

Risks will most likely require a diversity of interventions. It will typically take more than a single action to reduce a given risk. A creative and diverse approach is recommended, usually requiring a mix of interventions. This need is a sound rationale for coordination of partner actions.

On Opportunity and Opportunity Enhancement

Opportunities can outweigh residual risks. Even if risks remain, countries may cooperate if certain political opportunities or gains become apparent. Opportunity is therefore a powerful factor in determining the outcome of a cooperation offer and is an area for further study.

Politics is difficult to predict, so anticipation is critical. Laying the foundation for cooperation by reducing risks will prepare countries for deals. For partners engaging countries in cooperation, staying abreast of regional geopolitics is important, so when the time is ripe for cooperation, action can be taken.

National, regional, and global events all affect opportunities. Changes at any scale can create or change opportunity.

On Supporting Cooperation

Long-term time commitment is likely. Cooperation takes several years of planning and confidence building, often before negotiations even begin.

Deals are dynamic. Once a deal is reached, the situation does not become static. Deals can be fragile and fall apart, or evolve and grow into stronger and more sustainable arrangements. Accordingly, periodic assessments are needed to reflect a proper diagnosis of current realities.

Reference

World Bank. 2001. "Projects on International Waterways." Operational Policy statement 7.50, World Bank, Washington, DC.

Global Streams of Influence[1]

Introduction

Over the past century, international waters (IW) has emerged as an area of special attention within the field of water resources management. This attention is indeed warranted, given that there are over 260 international rivers (Wolf et al. 1999) and over 270 shared aquifers (UNESCO-IHP 2008). The topic has evolved following a shift in focus from navigation to non-navigational uses of rivers. Concurrently, scientific understanding of the complexity of hydrological processes, including the interconnectedness of surface and ground water, has deepened. Together, these factors have necessitated a broader and more integrated approach to water resources management, including locations where water intersects political boundaries. Because of the inherent political difficulties associated with IW, bilateral and multilateral agreements among co-riparians are increasingly being promoted to avert or mitigate conflicts. These agreements are typically supported by management frameworks that have been shaped by the global discourse on IW.

The salience of IW is demonstrated through targeted efforts by several countries and organizations that include their bilateral partners as well as global institutions, such as the United Nations (UN) agencies, the World Water Council, the Global Water Partnership (GWP), and the multilateral development banks. Additionally, IW is now finding a place in international events like the World Water Forum and the Stockholm World Water Week. Three major sources, or streams, of influence have contributed to the growing global awareness of IW: the development of international law, the emergence of the global environmental movement, and the inception and institutionalization of integrated water resources management (IWRM).[2]

- International water law has been developed and promoted by the UN and affiliated and unaffiliated international legal organizations, with the goal of establishing a common global legal framework recognized and adopted by sovereign nations. Since 1911, these organizations have attempted to set rules that balance state sovereignty with regional interests and "good neighbor" responsibilities.

- The global environmental movement has contributed concepts such as ecosystem health, the drainage basin, and integration. The UN has hosted global conferences to facilitate communication of these concepts and the drafting of plans for their adoption, beginning at Stockholm in 1972. International environmental organizations have also asserted influence through this stream. For example, the Global Environment Facility (GEF) has taken the lead in financing new IW initiatives through its support for the UN Development Programme (UNDP), the UN Environment Programme (UNEP), and World Bank–executed grants.

- Finally and most recently, IWRM has emerged as the new paradigm for water management at many levels, including the international river basin level. People and institutions associated with the IWRM stream have defined the concept of participatory basin level management and are institutionalizing it in countries and regions with the support of institutions such as the Global Water Partnership. The current discourse on IW has been informed and influenced by the debates around these three streams.

International Water Law: The Legal Stream

Demand for non-navigational uses of rivers, such as hydropower and irrigation, intensified in the first half of the 20th century (Elver 2006). Because previously established international water law was designed to deal solely with river navigation (Elver 2006; Salman 2007), no formula existed for addressing the emerging issue of competing uses. As states attempted to reconcile their differences on case-by-case bases, tensions became evident, particularly with respect to state sovereignty and riparian rights. In the early years, the only public approach taken by states depended almost exclusively on their own economic interests. For example, in 1895, the United States endorsed the principle of absolute sovereignty when Attorney General Judson Harmon announced that the United States was not obligated to consider how its upstream uses of the Rio Grande would affect Mexico downstream (Salman 2007). In contrast, riparians, who often preceded upstream states in riparian use (Beaumont 2000), tended to favor the principle of absolute territorial integrity, in which upstream states must defer to downstream users (Salman 2007). Even though both principles apply to international waters, both take a national rather than regional standpoint.

Beginning in 1911, a legal framework for international waters began to take form, due to the collective efforts of three organizations—the International Institute of Law (IIL), the International Law Association (ILA), and the International Law Commission (ILC). Collectively, these three organizations have formulated the bulk of global IW policy over the past century (see table A.1). The ILC is associated with the UN; the IIL and the ILA are well-respected scholarly organizations with no direct affiliation with sovereign states. Rules and resolutions established by these organizations are not legally binding unless adopted and ratified by the relevant states.

While the ILC has drafted many recent and formal proposed regimes pertaining to international waters, earlier and arguably equally influential work, including the Helskinki Rules, was undertaken by the ILA and the International Institute of Law. In 1911, the International Institute of Law issued the International Regulations Regarding the Use of International Watercourses for the Purposes other than Navigation, often referred to as the Madrid Declaration (Beaumont 2000). This declaration established the interdependent nature of co-riparians, as well as the earliest version of the principle of no significant harm, described as a state's obligation not to interfere unduly with co-riparian uses of a shared river (Teclaff 1996). Thus, the principle of absolute sovereignty, though never universally accepted, was at that time challenged in the global arena (Salman 2007), and the more conservative concept of limited territorial sovereignty became the universally recognized principle. The Madrid Declaration also set down a rule that the

Table A.1   Legal Influences and Associated Contributions, 1911–2008

Date	Legal influence	Major contribution(s) to IW
1911	Madrid Declaration	Interdependency; "no significant harm"; no modifying of "essential" river characteristics
1956	Dubrovnik Statement	"Equitable and reasonable use"
1958	New York Resolution	"Beneficial use"
1961	Salzburg Resolution	N/A
1966	Helsinki Rules	SW/GW connectivity; no priority of use; "no significant harm" not included as a separate provision
1982	Complementary Rules Applicable to International Water Resources (ILA)	Mitigation of impact; compensation for injury
1986	Rules on Transboundary Groundwater	Management of groundwater both connected and unconnected to surface water
1997	UN Watercourse Convention	Participation; information sharing; revived "no significant harm" but placed it as inferior to "equitable and reasonable use"
2000	Campione Consolidation	N/A
2004	Berlin Rules	Stated "no significant harm" and "equitable and reasonable use" are equal; applicable to domestic basins
2008	The Law on Transboundary Aquifers (ILC)	"Equitable and reasonable utilization" rather than "use"

Note: ILA = International Law Association; ILC = International Law Commission; SW = Surface Water; GW = Ground Water; N/A = not applicable.

essential characteristics of a shared river could not be seriously modified by use (Teclaff 1996), which may be regarded today as a reference to environmental sustainability.

In 1956, the ILA issued the Dubrovnik Statement, which confirmed sovereign state control over transboundary waters and at the same time emphasized consideration of impacts on co-riparians. This statement marked the emergence of the principle of equitable and reasonable use in international water policy (Salman 2007). The principle, which originated from riparian rights in Britain and Wales, was already being applied to dispute resolution within the United States (Beaumont 2000). Two years later, the ILA's New York Resolution refined the equitable and reasonable use to pertain specifically to beneficial uses. In 1961, the International Institute of Law adopted the Salzburg Resolution, which emphasized conjunctively equitable and reasonable use and no significant harm (Salman 2007). Finally, in 1966, the ILA attempted to incorporate many of these concepts into a concise set of rules when it formulated and adopted the Helsinki Rules on the Non-navigational Uses of International Watercourses (Helsinki Rules).

A number of riparian states accepted the Helsinki Rules, which served as the basis of several bilateral agreements (Dellapenna and Gupta 2008) and dispute settlements (Salman 2007). In the 1990s, the International Law Commission drafted its own set of similar rules. The Helsinki Rules rearticulated the principle of equitable and reasonable use (Dellapenna and Gupta 2009; Salman 2007; Teclaff 1996). It was also the first international legal framework to acknowledge the connection between surface water and groundwater (Salman 2007; Teclaff 1996) and to address navigational and non-navigational uses conjunctively, explicitly stating that no use takes inherent priority over another use (Salman 2007). Missing from the Helsinki Rules was a stand-alone provision on no significant harm (Salman 2007). This principle—as well as its relationship to other principles and its appropriateness in general—was continually debated in various legal and water-related forums over the next several decades.

Following its adoption of the Helsinki Rules, the ILA continued to explore the topic of international waters, first augmenting and then eventually consolidating the Helsinki Rules. In 1982, the ILA adopted the Complementary Rules Applicable to International Water Resources, which added provisions such as mitigation of harm and compensation for injury (Salman 2007). In 1986, the ILA adopted the Rules on Transboundary Groundwater, which applied to *all* groundwaters, not just those connected to surface waters, as was the case with the Helsinki Rules (Teclaff 1996). The ILA consolidated its work from the 1960s–1990s into a single set of rules. This document, the Campione Consolidation of the International Law Association Rules on International Water Resources, 1966–1999, was adopted in London in 2000 (Salman 2007).

Concurrently, at the request of the UN, the ILC drafted its own set of rules on shared waters. Over 25 years in the making, the UN Convention on the Non-navigational Uses of International Watercourses (Watercourse Convention) was finalized in 1997, although it has yet to be ratified or acceded to by the required number of states to enter into force. Even so, the Watercourse Convention has been used as a model for several interstate agreements, including the 2000 Revised Protocol on Shared Watercourses of the Southern African Development Community (SADC) (Beaumont 2000). The Watercourse Convention is generally regarded as the modern template for managing international rivers; however, the ILC chose not to include groundwater (Beaumont 2000). The ILA viewed this omission as a major flaw in the Watercourse Convention and subsequently drafted yet another set of rules itself (Salman 2007).

The Watercourse Convention includes principles of participation, cooperation, compensation for harm, data and information sharing, and attention to vital human needs (Beaumont 2000). Most significantly, it reiterates the principle of equitable and reasonable use from the Helsinki Rules and revives the principle of no significant harm from previous International Institute of Law and ILA frameworks (Beaumont 2000). Although the Convention sets forth both principles, analysis by legal experts suggests that the former takes precedence over the latter (Salman 2007). Indeed, the International Court of Justice (ICJ) endorsed this prioritization in 1997 when settling a dispute between Hungary and Slovakia over a dam on the Danube; the ICJ referred to the principle of equitable and reasonable use without referring to the principle of no significant harm.

Following the Watercourse Convention, it was apparent that a few issues still required attention—the integration of groundwater into international water law and the balance between the seemingly competing principles of equitable and reasonable use and no significant harm. Thus, the ILA revisited its Helsinki and subsequent Rules, altering language to address gaps and shortcomings (Salman 2007). In 2004, the ILA adopted the Berlin Rules on Water Resources (Dellapenna and Gupta 2008). The Berlin Rules made two contributions to global policy on international waters:

• It presented the two principles as equal, stating, "Basin States shall in their respective territories manage the waters of an international drainage basin in an equitable and reasonable manner having due regard for the obligation not to cause significant harm to other basin States (ILA 2004, article 12:1)."
• It integrated domestic and international water law, and so it was not limited in scope to international basins but also applicable to basins within a state (Dellapenna and Gupta 2008).

The most recent development in the legal stream was the ILC's 2008 adoption of its separate formulation pertaining to groundwater—the Law of Transboundary Aquifers (ILC 2008). The general principles of the Law of Transboundary Aquifers mirror those in the Watercourse Convention, with one minor, yet potentially significant, change in language: the principle of equitable and reasonable use from the Watercourse Convention has been changed to equitable and reasonable utilization (Eckstein 2007). According to Eckstein (2007), this alteration broadens the scope of the principle in that "use" relates only to the purpose for the water, while "utilization" also relates to the mechanism and methodology of that purpose (Eckstein 2007). In addition, though the principle of no significant harm is included, it was extensively debated, because assessing harm to aquifers is exponentially more complex than assessing harm to rivers (Eckstein 2007).

The Global Environmental Movement—The Environment Stream

The global environmental movement that began in the 1970s, primarily in developed countries, advanced a holistic approach to natural resources management that included water. As it became clear that water—particularly its degradation and scarcity—was a priority topic of concern, IW gained attention. It was already apparent that the paradigm of water management emphasizing economic growth and unilateral development was not a sustainable path forward (Elver 2006). The fragmented management of the past had proved environmentally damaging and unsustainable; thus, new management regimes that targeted ecosystems and drainage basins were proffered as alternatives. For IW, this eventually meant "joint management" and "integration" among co-riparians. The UN took the initial lead in the early 1970s, and others carried the baton in the 1990s (table A.2).

The UN held its first global environmental conference in 1972 in Stockholm—the Conference on the Human Environment. This was the first of a series of high-level conferences that the UN hosted over the next two decades (Biswas 2003). A major product of this conference was the Stockholm Declaration, a set of principles regarding the relationship between humans and the environment. The principles stressed the importance of sustainable development that emphasizes environmental and social dimensions as well as economic and integrated regional planning. Additional considerations include state sovereignty and the impacts on neighboring states (see UNCHE 1972). Most notably, the Stockholm Declaration advocates an ecosystems approach to natural resource management (Teclaff 1996), which set a precedent for managing water holistically, taking all uses into account.

In this same time frame, the UN's International Hydrological Decade was coming to a close. The International Hydrological Programme (IHP) was born out of this period of awareness, officially established under the UN Educational, Scientific, and Cultural Organization (UNESCO) in 1975 (Varady, Meehan, and McGovern 2009). Although the decade did

Table A.2   Environmental Influences and Associated Contributions, 1965–2002

Date	Environmental influence	Major contribution(s) to IW
1965	International Hydrological Decade	Global water awareness; the International Hydrology Programme (IHP) was launched later
1972	UN Stockholm—Human Environment	Ecosystems approach to resource management
1977	UN Mar del Plata—Water	Integrated planning for water management; systems approach
1991	Global Environment Facility (GEF) established; New instruments in 1994	Implementation mechanism for transboundary resource management, including water
1992	Dublin Conference on Water and Environment	River basin as management unit; integrated planning and development of shared waters; joint management
1992	UN Rio de Janeiro—Environment and Development	IWRM; holistic management; Global Water Partnership envisioned
2001	Bonn Conference on Freshwater	Harmony with nature
2002	UN Johannesburg—Sustainable Development	Promoted further implementation of Agenda 21, chapter 18

Note: the International Drinking Water Supply and Sanitation Decade 1981–90 focused primarily on a sector, rather than IW. UN = United Nations.

not make direct contributions to IW, today the IHP is involved in two relevant IW programs (UNESCO 2011) discussed in following sections.

In 1977, the UN hosted the Conference on Water in Mar del Plata, at which the UN presented the Mar del Plata Action Plan. Although the plan is not specific to international waters, it contained several relevant provisions in the recommendations section. Included among these was the first reference to integrated water resources management in a global setting: section D[3] calls for increased attention to integrated planning of water management (Falkenmark 1977), building on the integrated approach to general resource management advocated in the Stockholm Declaration, as well as a systems approach. Arguably, the most relevant provisions are contained in section H: International Cooperation, where principles that closely resemble those highlighted in the discussion of the legal stream can be found. These include the following (adapted from Falkenmark 1977; Beaumont 2000):

- Territorial sovereignty
- Equality
- The duality of both sovereign right to use resources and the duty to not cause harm to neighbors
- Equitable utilization of resources to promote solidarity and cooperation.

The growing interest in transboundary environmental issues led to the creation of the Global Environment Facility (GEF) by the global community in 1991. The GEF was tasked with promoting international cooperation around environmental protection in six areas, including international waters (Gerlak 2004) within the context of overall water resources management. By 1994, the GEF was serving as a funding mechanism for environmental projects and services, relying on the World Bank, the UNDP, and the UNEP for project implementation (Gerlak 2004).

In 1992, the UN held the Conference on the Environment and Development in Rio de Janeiro. Water scarcity was one of the four target issue areas that the conference addressed (UNDPI 1997). The conference stimulated the drafting of Agenda 21, a framework to guide global resource management. Chapter 18 outlines seven program areas for freshwater, and IWRM is the first on the first. Section A of Chapter 18 advocates holistic management and integrated management, including basin-wide joint management of shared water resources (UNCED 1992a). A complementary document, the Rio Declaration, echoes the core resource management principles found in the Stockholm Declaration, the Mar del Plata Action Plan, and several international legal frameworks targeting water. Principles 2 and 3 of the Rio Declaration refer to the concepts of state sovereignty, equitable use, and the obligation to not cause harm (UNCED 1992b).

In preparation for the Rio conference, a large group of experts convened four months earlier in Dublin to discuss water and make appropriate recommendations for the agenda. This meeting, the International Conference of Water and the Environment (ICWE), produced the Dublin Statement on Water and the Environment (Dublin Statement). Like Agenda 21, the ICWE's major contribution to global water policy was in promoting IWRM. The Dublin Statement advocated the river basin as the unit of management, as well as integrated planning and development of transboundary water resources (ICWE 1992). In addition, it specifically encouraged fostering joint integrated water management institutions (Giordano and Wolf 2003). The Dublin Principles emphasizing management at the lowest appropriate level, participation of civil society, and water as an economic good remains of interest to this day.

Clearly, 1992 was a pivotal year for international waters in general and for the development of the IWRM concept in particular. The Dublin conference was the first international event in 15 years to specifically address global water concerns and to strongly promote IWRM.

The Rio conference was the first intergovernmental meeting at which IWRM was formally discussed (Savenije and Van der Zaag 2008) and also where the idea for a global water council to implement IWRM was born[4] (WWC 2010).

Two additional influential events in the environmental stream took place a decade later—the International Conference on Freshwater in Bonn (2001) and the UN World Summit on Sustainable Development in Johannesburg (2002). Bonn, like Dublin a decade earlier, was a preparatory meeting for the latter (Rahaman and Varis 2005). The major output of the Bonn conference was the Bonn Keys, a document that in essence summarizes the conference's recommendations for action. One of the five Bonn Keys promotes cooperation and harmony with nature in water management, including transboundary basins (FMENCNS 2001).

The Johannesburg conference in 2002, which advocated IWRM at all levels, did not directly address international waters (UN 2002). One of the most significant contributions was the Johannesburg Ministerial Declaration, in which delegates not only reaffirmed commitment to Agenda 21, but also encouraged the UN to further its implementation (Giordano and Wolf 2003). Another was its call for IWRM plans at the country level.

The Inception and Institutionalization of IWRM—The IWRM Stream

Immediately following the Rio conference, international water resources organizations and programs expanded (Giordano and Wolf 2003). Concepts and approaches to water management that had surfaced through the environmental stream were institutionalized, profoundly affecting the world view of shared waters. These institutions constitute the third stream of influence (table A.3).

Starting in the 1990s, pivotal international water organizations began to emerge, including the GWP[5] and the World Water Council (WWC) (Savinije and Van der Zaag 2008). The GWP and the WWC, both established in 1996, are involved in advocacy and global implementation of IWRM principles and practices (Savinije and Van der Zaag 2008). The WWC focuses at a higher level on raising political awareness, namely through the World Water Forums, while the GWP aids implementation at the regional and national levels through its 13 Regional Water Partnerships and 74 Country Water Partnerships (GWP 2010; Varady, Meehan, and McGovern 2009).

Table A.3   IWRM Influences and Associated Contributions, 1991–2009

Date	IWRM institutional influence	Major contributions to IW
1991	Global Environment Facility	International Waters (IW) focal area; funds implementation of joint management and institutional reforms
1996	Global Water Partnership	Ownership of integrated water resources management (IWRM); Regional Water Partnerships that emphasize joint management
1996	World Water Council	Triennial World Water Forums, 1997-present
1996	International Water Management Institute	Research on transboundary waters, in particular in the developing world
1997	Stockholm International Water Institute	Annual World Water Weeks in Stockholm; shared waters as theme in 2009
2003	United Nations Water	Open access forum for information exchange; task force on IW; implementation of Agenda 21, chapter 18
2003	World Water Assessment Program	Triennial World Water Development Reports
2009	From Potential Conflict to Cooperation Potential and International Shared Aquifer Resource Management programs (through the International Hydrological Programme and the World Water Assessment Program)	Capacity building in transboundary management; technical assessments of international aquifer basins

In 1997, the WWC hosted the first World Water Forum in Marrakech. These forums have continued every three years since, with the topic of international waters demonstrating a general pattern of increasing importance at the forums. The Hague Forum in 2000 was guided by the WWC's 2000 Vision Report (WWC 2000), which advocated IWRM, including attention to cooperation over international waters (Biswas 2003). In its section on international cooperation, the report highlighted several key concepts (adapted from WWC 2000):

- Regional institutions, such as river basin organizations
- Trust building efforts
- Binding agreements
- Dispute resolution mechanisms.

The Ministerial Declaration following The Hague Forum stated that "sharing waters" was one of seven challenges to achieving water security in the 21st century (Giordano and Wolf 2003); following Kyoto in 2003, the Ministerial Declaration stated that cooperation over transboundary waters was one of 29 important policy areas (WWC 2003). After the forum in Mexico City in 2006, a report titled "Implementing IWRM" emphasized river basin organizations and regional decision making, while also advocating dispute resolution mechanisms, data sharing, and integrating groundwater into regional plans (WWC 2006). International waters became even more integrated into the agenda at the next, and most recent, forum. In Istanbul in 2009, Basin Management and Transboundary Cooperation was one of 23 sub-themes, which included dialogues over sustainability, equity, stakeholder involvement, and operational tools (WWC 2010). The next forum is scheduled for 2012 in Marseille; one of the 12 priority action areas is to "contribute to cooperation and peace through water" (WWC 2011). Sub-themes include increasing the number of bilateral and multilateral agreements, fostering joint management institutions, training decision makers in transboundary water management and conflict resolution, and developing information sharing mechanisms (WWC 2011).

The GWP's primary influence has been to promote IWRM, in particular, its applicability at a variety of scales. The GWP formulated a broad framework for implementation that relies on policies, institutions, and management instruments for success (GWP 2008). This framework is complemented by a well-received toolbox of IWRM practices. International waters is integrated throughout GWP's approach to IWRM, in particular, through river basin organizations and conflict management mechanisms. This emphasis has facilitated appropriate river basin management practices at the country level. In addition, the Regional Water Partnerships specifically emphasize the management of international waters (GWP 2010).

In addition to the GWP and WWC, the International Water Management Institute (IWMI)[6] and the Stockholm International Water Institute (SIWI), both research organizations with a freshwater focus, were founded in the mid-1990s. World Water Week, an annual conference for decision makers, collaborating organizations, and academics, has been hosted by SIWI since its inception in 1997[7] (SIWI 2011). The purpose of these meetings is to "provide an annual focal point for solutions to the growing array of water and development challenges facing the world (SIWI 2009)." In 2009, transboundary waters was the "special focus" of World Water Week (SIWI 2009).

The GEF has played a major role in the promotion of international waters by funding relevant projects and programs. Its primary purpose is to provide a mechanism for implementing global environmental goals, and it has grown into the largest multilateral source of aid specifically targeting the global environment (Gerlak 2004). In 1995, the GEF released its operational strategy containing the long-term goal for its international waters focal area—to support the joint management of international waters (GEF 2010). GEF's international waters program subsequently moved into full operational mode in support of institutional reforms, investments, and joint management of rivers, aquifers, and oceans (GEF 2010).

In 2003, UN Water succeeded an existing network of global water agencies in response to a growing need for a coherent, coordinated approach to address a plethora of interrelated freshwater issues (UN Water 2009). UN Water is the official UN mechanism for following up on water-related decisions by the 2002 World Summit in Johannesburg (UN Water 2008). Within UN Water, six task forces were initially created, one of which is Transboundary Waters (UN Water 2009). UN Water serves as a platform for information exchange (UN Water 2009), while alternate UN organizations and programs target specific challenges or sectors. For example, the World Water Assessment Program (WWAP) and the International Hydrological Programme (IHP) are both involved in international waters; over the past decade, WWAP and IHP have taken on the From Potential Conflict to Cooperation Potential (FPCCP) and the International Shared Aquifer Resource Management (ISARM) programs under UNESCO. FPCCP is a research and capacity building program that fosters cooperation and joint development of international waters; ISARM is a technical program that is developing a global inventory of international aquifer basins and guidance tools for the management of aquifers (UNESCO 2011). IHP frequently coordinates with GEF's international waters program and was also a contributor to the International Law Commission's Rules on Transboundary Aquifers (UNESCO 2011).

The WWAP has triennially published the *World Water Development Report* since 2003 (UN Water 2009). The 2009 report, *Water in a Changing World*, addresses international waters in the context of impending scarcity, degraded water quality, and potential basin closure, highlighting the importance of cooperation and data exchange to achieve a more sustainable future (WWAP 2009). The fourth report (2012) has the overarching theme of "managing water under uncertainty and risk" (WWAP 2011), reflecting the current resource management approaches of resilience and adaptability.

Figure A.1   Timeline of Events along the Three Streams of Influence

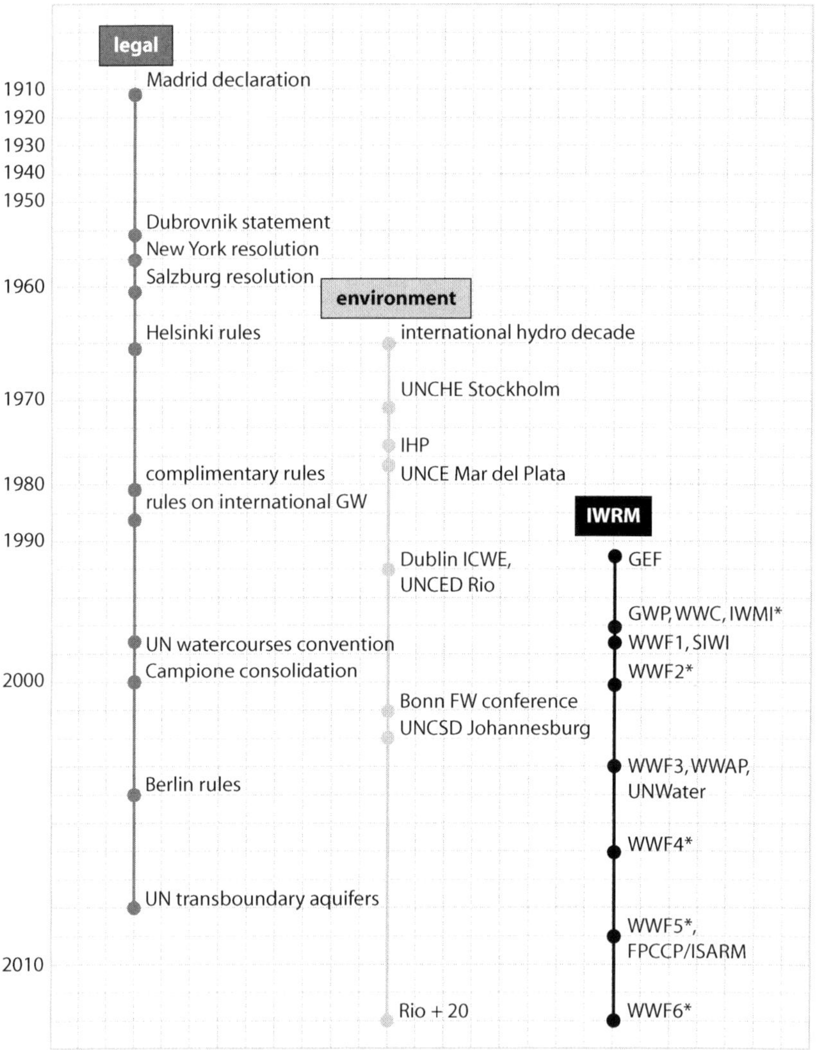

Note: (+) IWMI replaced IIMI (established in 1984); IIMI focused on irrigation rather than international waters. (*)
Denotes World Water Forums that specifically targeted (or will target) IW. GEF = Global Environment Facility;
GWP = Global Water Partnership; ICWE = International Conference on Water and Environment; IHP = International
Hydrological Programme; IWMI = International Water Management Institute; SIWI = Stockholm International
Water Institute; UN = United Nations; UNCED = UN Conference on the Environment and Development;
UNCHE = UN Conference on the Human Environment; UNCSD = UN Conference on Sustainable Development;
WWAP = World Water Assessment Program; WWC = World Water Council.

Conclusion

The cause of international waters has developed through three interweaving streams of influence—the legal, environmental, and IWRM. Figure A.1 illustrates a comprehensive timeline. The cause seemed to disappear during the 1980s, but has since been emphasized rather consistently through all three streams in the 1990s, and does not appear to be losing momentum. The fact that the World Water Forum in Marseille lists cooperation over international waters as one of 12 priority action areas corroborates this notion, as does the GEF's revised and augmented international waters strategy published in 2010.[8] Also, SIWI's Water Week focused on international waters in 2009; the Bonn 2011 Conference emphasized the IWRM agenda through water energy linkages. In fact, 2012–13 should be a telling year for international waters—in addition to the upcoming World Water Forum, the Rio +20 Conference on Sustainable Development, as well as the annual World Water Weeks in Stockholm that are also expected to highlight IW.

Notes

1. Comments on an earlier version of this note from Torkil Jonch Clausen, Charles de Liva, Al Duda, and Ivan Zavasky are acknowledged with appreciation.

2. The IWRM stream was also inspired by Rio 1992 and the Johannesburg World Summit on Sustainable Development (WSSD) Plan of Implementation.

3. Mar del Plata Action Plan on the World's Water Resources: Recommendations: Section D. Policy Planning and Management, "Increased attention should be paid to the integrated planning of water management. Integrated policies and legislative and administrative guidelines are needed so as to ensure a good adaptation of resources to needs and reduce, if necessary, the risk of serious supply shortages and ecological damage, to ensure public acceptance of planned water schemes and to ensure their financing. Particular consideration should be given not only to the cost-effectiveness of planned water schemes, but also to ensuring optimal social benefits of water resources use, as well as to the protection of human health and the environment as a whole. Attention should also be paid to the shift from single-purpose to multipurpose water resources development as the degree of development of water resources and water use in river basins increases...." (from Falkenmark 1977: 223).

4. This was a motivation behind the establishment of the World Water Council four years later (WWC 2010).

5. GWP was greatly influenced by the Dublin Principles.

6. IWMI transitioned from the International Irrigation Management Institute (IIMI) at this time.

7. World Water Week is the successor to the previous Stockholm Water Symposiums, hosted by the municipal water and wastewater provider in Stockholm since 1991, until SIWI took over in 1997 (SIWI 2011).

8. The GEF published its Focal Area Strategies for its fifth replenishment in 2010, which included a revised and augmented strategy for its international waters program (GEF 2010).

References

Beaumont, P. 2000. "The 1997 UN Convention on the Law of Non-navigational Uses of International Watercourses: Its Strengths and Weaknesses from a Water Management Perspective and the Need for New Workable Guidelines." *Water Resources Development* 16 (4): 475–95.

Biswas, A. K. 2003. "From Mar del Plata to Kyoto: An Analysis of Global Water Policy Dialogues." Third World Center for Water Management. http://www.doccentre.net/docsweb/water1/water-biswas.htm.

Dellapenna, J., and J. Gupta. 2008. "Toward Global Law on Water." *Global Governance* 14: 437–53.

Eckstein, G. E. 2007. "Commentary on the UN International Law Commission's draft articles on the Law of Transboundary Aquifers." *Colorado Journal of International Environmental Law and Policy* 18 (3): 537–610.

Elver, H. 2006. "International Environmental Law, Water, and the Future." *Third World Quarterly* 27 (5): 885–901.

Falkenmark, M. 1977. "UN Water Conference: Agreement on Goals and Action Plan." *Ambio* 6 (4): 222–27.

FMENCN (Federal Ministry for the Environment, Nature Conservation, and Nuclear Safety). 2001. International Conference on Freshwater, Bonn, Final Report, December 3–7. http://www.bmu.de/english/water_management/doc/3468.php.

Gerlak, A. K. 2004. "One Basin at a Time: The Global Environment Facility and Governance of Transboundary Waters." *Global Environmental Politics* 4 (4): 108–41.

Giordano, M. A., and A. T. Wolf. 2003. "Sharing Waters: Post-Rio International Water Management." *Natural Resources Forum* 27: 163–71.

GEF (Global Environment Facility). 2010. "International Waters Strategy. Focal Area Strategies (for the fifth replenishment)." http://www.thegef.org/gef/GEF5_InternationalWaters_Strategy.

GWP (Global Water Partnership). 2008. "Toolbox: Integrated Water Resources Management." http://www.gwptoolbox.org.

———. 2010. "Regional Water Partnerships." http://www.gwp.org/en/About-GWP/ The-network/Regional-Water-Partnerships.

ICWE (International Conference on Water and the Environment). 1992. "The Dublin Statement on Water and Sustainable Development. Republished online by the United Nations." http://www.un-documents.net/h2o-dub.htm.

ILA (International Law Association). 2004. "Berlin Conference: Water Resources Law." ILA, Berlin, August.

ILC (International Law Commission). 2008. Draft Articles on the Law of Transboundary Aquifers. http://untreaty.un.org/ilc/texts/instruments/english/ draft%20articles/8_5_2008.pdf.

Rahaman, M. M., and O. Varis. 2005. "Integrated Water Resources Management: Evolution, Prospects, and Future Challenges." *Sustainability: Science, Practice and Policy* 1(1). http://sspp.proquest.com/archives/vol1iss1/0407–03 .rahaman.html.

Salman, M. A. S. 2007. "The Helsinki Rules, the UN Watercourses Convention and the Berlin Rules: Perspectives on International Water Law." *Water Resources Development* 23 (4): 625–40.

Savenije, H. H. G., and P. Van der Zaag. 2008. "Integrated Water Resources Management: Concepts and Issues." *Physics and Chemistry of the Earth* 33: 290–97.

SIWI (Stockholm International Water Institute). 2009. "World Water Week: Overarching Conclusions, 2009." http://www.worldwaterweek.org/documents/ Resources/Synthesis/Overarching_Conclusions_2009.pdf.

———. 2011. "About SIWI." http://www.siwi.org/about.

Teclaff, L. A. 1996. "Evolution of the River Basin Concept in National and International Water Law." *Natural Resources Journal* 36: 359–91.

UN (United Nations). 2002. Implementation Plan for the World Summit on Sustainable Development. http://www.un.org/esa/sustdev/documents/ WSSD_POI_PD/English/WSSD_PlanImpl.pdf.

UNCHE (United Nations Conference on the Human Environment). 1972. Stockholm Declaration. http://www.unep.org/Documents.multilingual/ Default.asp?documentid=97.

UNCED (United Nations Conference on the Environment and Development). 1992a. Agenda 21. http://www.un.org/esa/sustdev/documents/agenda21/ english/Agenda21.pdf.

———. 1992b. Report of the United Nations Conference on the Environment and Development, Annex 1: Rio Declaration on the Environment and

Development. http://www.un.org/documents/ga/conf151/aconf15126-1annex1.htm.

UNDPI (United Nations Department of Public Information). 1997. "Earth Summit. UN Briefing Papers: the World Conferences: Developing Priorities for the 21st Century." http://www.un.org/geninfo/bp/enviro.html.

UNESCO (United Nations Educational, Scientific and Cultural Organization). 2011. "International Hydrological Programme: IHP programs." http://www.unesco.org/new/en/natural-sciences/environment/water/ihp/ihp-programmes.

UNESCO-IHP. 2008. Inventory of Transboundary Aquifers. http://www.crcnetbase.com/doi/abs/10.1201/b11062-23.

UN Water. 2008. "Transboundary Waters: Sharing Benefits, Sharing Responsibilities. Report by the Task Force on Transboundary Waters." http://www.unwater.org/downloads/UNW_TRANSBOUNDARY.pdf.

———. 2009. "Discover UN Water." http://www.unwater.org/discover.html.

Varady, R. G., K. Meehan, and E. McGovern. 2009. "Charting the Emergence of 'Global Water Initiatives' in World Water Governance." *Physics and Chemistry of the Earth* 34: 150–55.

Wolf, A. T., J. A. Natharius, J. J. Danielson, B. S. Ward, and J. K. Pender. 1999. "International River Basins of the World." *International Journal of Water Resources Development* 15 (4): 387–427.

WWAP (World Water Assessment Program). 2009. *World Water Development Report*, 3rd ed. http://www.unesco.org/water/wwap.

———. 2011. About the World Water Development Report, Fourth Edition. http://www.unesco.org/water/wwap/wwdr.

WWC (World Water Council). 2000. "World Water Vision Commission Report: A Water Secure World." WWC, Marseille.

———. 2003. "The Third World Water Forum Ministerial Declaration." Ministry of Foreign Affairs, Japan. http://www.mofa.go.jp/policy/environment/wwf/declaration.html.

———. 2006. "Local Actions for a Global Challenge: Implementing IWRM." Report from the 4th World Water Forum, Mexico City. http://www.worldwaterforum4.org.mx/uploads/TBL_DOCS_79_43.pdf.

———. 2010. "About Us: Background." http://www.worldwatercouncil.org/index.php?id=92.

———. 2011. "Sixth World Water Forum." http://www.worldwaterforum6.org.